TAKING *on* GOLIATH

How To Unleash The David In All Of Us

ROB MARSHALL

TAKING ON GOLIATH

Copyright © 2006 Rob Marshall. All rights reserved.

No part of this publication may be reproduced or transmitted in any form or by any means, mechanical or electronic, including photocopying and recording, or by any information storage and retrieval system, without permission in writing from author or publisher (except by a reviewer, who may quote brief passages and/or show brief video clips in a review).

ISBN: 1-933596-59-7 (Paperback)

ISBN: 1-60037-027-6 (Hardcover)

ISBN: 1-60037-040-3 (Audio)

ISBN: 1-60037-028-4 (eBook)

Published by:

MORGAN · JAMES
THE ENTREPRENEURIAL PUBLISHER

Morgan James Publishing, LLC
1225 Franklin Ave Ste 325
Garden City, NY 11530-1693
Toll Free 800-485-4943
www.MorganJamesPublishing.com

Habitat for Humanity®
Peninsula Building Partner

Cover & Interior Design by:
Heather Kirk
www.GraphicsByHeather.com
Heather@GraphicsByHeather.com

Cover Art by:
Gregory Marshall
© 2005 Gregory Marshall
www.Gregory-Marshall.com

All scripture quotations, unless otherwise indicated, are taken from the New King James Version®. Copyright © 1982 by Thomas Nelson, Inc. Used by permission. All rights reserved.

To my younger brother Peter, whose life showed me the meaning and the blessings of being a true servant.

Acknowledgements

So many people have an impact on a book when it's being written and revised, and I'm grateful to everyone who helped me. I especially want to thank the following people:

Ken Heath, Bonnie Ward-Muller, Bill Watson, Bert Rich, Matthew Marshall, Marjorie Thomas, Valerie Marshall, Elizabeth Keller, Elaine Flory, and Lois Earle, who read the early manuscripts and gave me feedback and encouragement.

My son Greg Marshall for taking the time to listen to my suggestions and corrections when he designed the cover art.

Heather Kirk, Norma Strange, Jeanette Barnes, David Hancock, and all the folks at Morgan James Publishing who believed in this project and helped make this book a reality.

Les Brown — mentor, coach, and master motivator — who encouraged me, believed in my gifts more than I did, and taught me how to follow my dreams.

My coaches — Lisa Jimenez, Scott Armstrong, and Alden Komorowski — for their faith in me, their encouragement, and their practical guidance.

The greatest speakers on the planet, the members of the Les Brown Speakers Network — especially Art Doakes, Steve Duncanson, Valorie Parker, Trice Atkinson, and Lauren Hudson.

Those who have influenced me and may not know it: Jim Rohn, Mike Litman, Armand Morin, John Childers, Frank McKinney, Dr. John P. Hayes, and Zig Ziglar.

My editors, Mary Jo Tate and Jeannine Gerace, for removing all those extra commas and helping me clarify the content of this book.

I also want to especially thank my wife, Dana, who has loved and supported me through all my trials and triumphs. She read and re-read the chapters of this book, and her comments and guidance helped make the book better than I could have made it on my own.

I am grateful to God, who helps me defeat all the Goliaths I face as I pursue His will for my life.

Table Of Contents

Foreword xi

Introduction xv

1 CLARITY — Preparing Our Hearts 1
    Preparing Our Hearts 6
    Written in Our Hearts 8
    The Desires of Our Hearts 12
    Taking Action 18

2 CHALLENGE — Learning to be Faithful 21
    David Had Been Faithful 25
    Seeing His Faithfulness 28
    Circumstance or Challenge? 30
    Taking Action 33

3 CONSEQUENCES — Risks and Rewards 35
    The Process, the Price, and the Prize 39
    Knowing the Prize is Right 41
    What Are the Risks? 43
    Focus on the Desired Outcome 45
    Taking Action 47

4 CONFRONTATION — Handling Criticism 51
    Who's Influencing Whom? 56
    Finding Diamonds in the Rough 60
    Taking Action 64

5 CONFIDENCE — Learning to Trust 67
    The Lion and the Bear 72

    Faith and Patience 76
    Taking Action 80

6 CREATIVITY — Using Our Imagination 83
    Saul's Armor 91
    Nothing New Under the Sun 94
    Five Smooth Stones 96
    Taking Action 99

7 COMMITMENT — Making Decisions 103
    The Acorn and the Oak Tree 110
    A Sense of Urgency 112
    Through the Finish Line 116
    Taking Action 119

8 COURAGE — Facing Our Fears 121
    Fear Versus Faith 130
    Today Versus Tomorrow 133
    Sowing Seeds 138
    Taking Action 140

9 CELEBRATION — Rejoicing in Achievement 143
    Great Blessings 150
    The Journey 152
    Thankful in Advance 154
    Taking Action 156

10 THE CONQUERING LIFE 159
    David After Goliath 165
    Repentance and Forgiveness 167

Knowing God's Will 170
Keeping His Commandments 172

Appendix **175**
1 Samuel 17 175

Notes **181**

Bonus **183**

Foreword

When I began to chase my dream and walk boldly in my greatness, I faced a multi-billion dollar industry full of Ivy League educated, former high-level corporate money makers with impressive letters behind their names.

I had none of that.

I was a former door-to-door salesman, a former radio guy, a former sanitation worker. I had no college degree, had, in fact, been labeled retarded as a child.

Yes, I know what it is like to face something that seems bigger than you and more powerful. And still prevail.

I have my own David and Goliath story.

In this book full of expert advice and practical tips, Rob Marshall helps readers stand up to the Goliaths in their own lives.

Rob's book has what so many other books lack: clarity. This book is full of clear steps to slay giants in your own life. It is also written in a way that engages and doesn't confuse. Rob uses his own experiences to make points, but this book does not become a personal story. Rather, he makes the reader confident that he speaks from a place of experience. This author builds a Biblical foundation for accomplishing mighty feats.

As you'll see in this book, beating the odds isn't always easy. In fact, Rob shows that it most often is anything but easy. But he doesn't leave you with just that. Even as he paints a realistic picture of what you may face, he never leaves you without the assurance that perseverance pays off. Perseverance and faith are integral to climbing the mountains in our lives.

Rob reminds us that, even as we strive to go higher, it's important to do a good job where we find ourselves — even in those jobs we think are "nothing jobs." God wants us to do well at each stage of our lives, not just in the things we like. Many people miss this point, as they sloppily complete tasks they don't deem worthy, but are necessary all the same. In *Taking on Goliath: How to Unleash the David in All of Us*, we see how even small things can have a huge impact.

Rob shows us that slacking in small tasks can condition us to be that way in the big deals of life. He shows us how a new attitude about how we approach seemingly unimportant things can help us do better in that which we deem the most important. This concept can positively change entire families, churches, businesses and even communities.

How are the little things in your life affecting the big things?

Taking on Goliath is a book about priorities and using what you have to get what you want. Just like David, each of us has frailties and challenges. But most people allow those shortcomings to sideline them. The young David though, when he took on the powerful giant Goliath, didn't allow his "lacks" to intimidate him. Instead, he used what was before him — a slingshot and a rock. What are the slingshots and rocks in your life you can use to get the better of a giant of a situation?

If you're not certain, then Rob's book will give you the clarity of vision to see how you are equipped right now to take your life to the next level. Rob will build your confidence, help you change your mindset, and equip you with tools to tackle your toughest challenges.

I've read many books on personal empowerment and self motivation, but this one stands apart as a true and effective combination of both. Get ready to discover the path to your greatest self.

Rob Marshall is a good guide.

Just as I was able to prevail against the Goliaths of my life and become one of the best known and most successful speakers in the business, so can you succeed against what seem to be insurmountable odds in your life. With the proper tools, you can defeat the giant.

Go on, let Rob show you how to slay your own Goliath!

~ Les Brown

INTRODUCTION

It was one of those days. Maybe you've experienced days like it as well — days when you feel like you have promised more than you could ever deliver. It was easy to be bold and announce to everybody what God was going to do for you, but now you're not so sure. Suddenly, you find yourself standing in a field all alone, face to face with an angry giant, and all you have in your hands are a sling and a few lousy pebbles. The question that keeps going through your mind is: "What was I thinking?"

> *The question that we need to answer is: How do we unleash the "David" that is in all of us?*

I don't know if that's how David felt, but I know that I've felt that way a number of times. I was just following my heart and doing what I thought God wanted me to do, and all along the path to my dream were giants, one after another. Maybe you've also felt like that on the way to your dreams. Not only do the problems not go away, but they also seem to get bigger and bigger. You wonder if you've made a mistake, and if anyone will notice as you quietly slip away, go back to your "day job," and forget the whole thing.

Even people who don't know much about the Bible have heard the story of David and Goliath. Newspaper and magazine stories tell us about modern-day Davids going up against Goliaths of all kinds. From business to politics, the little guys are facing some pretty big giants. The odds may be against them, but because of David's victory over Goliath, they believe they can win.

Throughout our lives we all face "giants" — problems and struggles that stand in our way. They loom large on the path to our dreams and make us feel like the difficulties are greater than the rewards. Because of David's example, however, we have hope — not that the problems will disappear, but that the problems we're facing can be overcome. Regardless of what others may think, we know from our own experiences with God that the victory doesn't go to the one who seems strongest but to the one who is willing to believe.

The story of David and Goliath is one of my favorites because David is a hero to whom I can relate. He has some major faults, but he has learned to trust God. Just as God worked in David's life, He's working in ours. It's not about having it all together, because David definitely didn't have it all together.

The question that we need to answer is: How do we unleash the "David" that is in all of us? What was it about David that enabled him to defeat Goliath? The answer is pretty simple. Jesus said, "Have faith in God" (Mk. 11:22). As simple as that answer may seem, putting that statement into practice and living a life that exemplifies faith in God isn't always as easy as it sounds.

In this story, we'll find some characteristics that appear repeatedly in the Bible and in the lives of people who have faith in God. As we look at them, we can ask ourselves how we're doing in each area. We'll find that we're doing well with some of them, but that others need work. And we'll learn from David's life that we can trust God to bring about the circumstances we need, when we need them, to help us grow in these key areas and in our faith in Him.

Then when we come face to face with yet another "giant," we'll realize that God has been using our struggles to teach us more about Himself. We'll understand that all things work for our good, even if some of the situations we had to endure were difficult and painful. We'll recognize that every victory, no matter how small, has strengthened our faith. Like David, we'll know that we can face the Goliaths in life because God is with us.

CHAPTER 1

Clarity — Preparing Our Hearts

Chapter 1

Clarity — Preparing Our Hearts

The LORD has sought for Himself a man after His own heart, and the LORD has commanded him to be commander over His people... ~ 1 Samuel 13:14

Then Samuel took the horn of oil and anointed him in the midst of his brothers; and the Spirit of the LORD came upon David from that day forward. ~ 1 Samuel 16:13

It takes a long time to become an overnight success. Because we rarely see the preparation and sacrifice that people go through, it can be easy to think that success just happens. Top athletes know that in order to win, they must continually hone their skills. They have to develop the mental and physical stamina needed in order to endure the hours of training and overcome the discouragement and challenges they'll face along the way. It's no different in any pursuit we might choose

> *It takes a long time to become an overnight success.*

At times we might assume that success is a matter of luck. We might say, "He was just in the right place at the right time." Looking at the story of David and Goliath, we could think it was like that for David. Personally, I'm not sure there's anything "right" about the place or timing when you're facing a giant who wants to kill you. But for us, just like it was for David, it's not just about being in the right place at the right time; we also have to be the right person in that place and time.

When we first meet David, Samuel the prophet has been sent to David's hometown of Bethlehem and to David's father Jesse. God told Samuel that he was to anoint one of Jesse's sons as the next king of Israel. Because he was worried that King Saul would kill him, Samuel pretended to be in town for a sacrifice and told Jesse that he and all his sons were invited to join him.

When Samuel met Jesse's sons, he saw the oldest son and said to himself, "Surely, the Lord's anointed is before Him!" (1 Sam. 16:6). But God spoke to Samuel and told him, "Do not look at his appearance or at his physical stature, because I have refused him. For the LORD does not see as man sees; for man looks at the outward appearance, but the LORD looks at the heart" (1 Sam. 16:7).

And so it went for all seven of Jesse's sons who were at the sacrifice. Samuel was a little confused when God didn't choose any of them, so he asked Jesse if he had any other sons. Then Jesse said something like, "Oh yeah . . . I do have one more, the youngest. But he's out taking care of the sheep."

I find it interesting that David wasn't with his brothers at the sacrifice. Did they forget to tell David about the invitation? Was he such a good shepherd that his father didn't feel comfortable leaving the sheep with anyone else? Did David get the invitation but ask to be excused

Chapter 1: Clarity

because he was too busy with the herd? Or was it because he was the youngest and least important of Jesse's sons? We really don't know.

When David finally joins them, we find out that he was just a young man, who probably wasn't old enough and definitely wasn't big and strong enough to even be in the army, let alone to command it. He certainly wasn't the person anyone would have chosen to be king. He didn't have the knowledge or experience to be king and he certainly didn't know the right people. And as the youngest in his family, he didn't have the position, money, or influence to do much of anything. Basically, David was a nobody.

There may be times when we look at our current circumstances and think that there isn't much we can do. We assume that the things we want and that God wants for our lives are just too hard to achieve where we are right now. We feel that the right opportunity won't come our way because we lack all the "important" stuff like knowledge, skills, connections, influence and money. But as we'll see from David's life, those aren't the most important things, because with God, all things are possible.

I don't know exactly what David had been doing all those days, weeks, and months while tending his father's sheep. But whatever it was, when God looked at his heart, He said, "This is the next king of Israel." David's father and brothers probably assumed that David would take over the family business and be a lowly shepherd for the rest of his life. But David apparently had other ideas, because he'd spent his time preparing his heart for something more.

Preparing Our Hearts

In 1 Samuel 13 we find out why God took the kingdom away from Saul. Saul panicked when he saw that the Philistines were gathering to attack him and that all his soldiers were running away. In desperation he made a burnt offering, which, according to God's laws, he wasn't allowed to do. Like most of us when we get scared and desperate, he made bad decisions. Rather than trusting God, we take matters into our own hands and usually make things worse.

When Samuel arrived, he asked Saul what he'd done. Unfortunately, Saul started making excuses and even tried to shift part of the blame to Samuel for having arrived later than originally planned. Then Saul said, "I felt compelled, and offered a burnt offering." (1 Sam. 13:12) Samuel replied: "You have done foolishly. You have not kept the commandment of the LORD your God, which He commanded you. For now the LORD would have established your kingdom over Israel forever. But now your kingdom shall not continue. The LORD has sought for Himself a man after His own heart, and the LORD has commanded him to be commander over His people, because you have not kept what the LORD commanded you" (1 Sam. 13:13-14).

> *God wants our hearts to be tender enough that we will regret and repent of our sin but tough enough that we pick ourselves up and keep moving toward our dreams even after we've failed.*

One thing we learn about David from this statement is that God called him "a man after His own heart." What does it mean to be "after God's own heart?" From what the Bible tells us about David's life, we know that it doesn't mean he was perfect. In fact he was far from it. Part of what it means is that David's heart was open to God. Later in his life when he sinned and God confronted him, he quickly admitted his sin and sought God's forgiveness.

In preparing our hearts, we can learn from David's example. The tendency is for us to react like Saul did, making excuses and trying to shift the blame. Admitting that we're wrong is hard for us to do. If we go back to the Garden of Eden when Adam and Eve sinned, we learn that it's in our nature to shift the blame. We try to make it look like we are just "innocent" victims, that someone else is at fault and there is nothing we can do.

Learning to be open and honest about our faults and failings is one of the fundamentals we need to master. Being able to admit that we've blown it without giving up altogether gives us the proper combination of humility and tenacity that God is looking for in our hearts. God wants our hearts to be tender enough that we will regret and repent of our sin, but tough enough that we pick ourselves up and keep moving toward our dreams even after we've failed.

How do we prepare our hearts? I really like what David wrote in Psalm 139. He tells us God knows everything there is to know about us. We can't hide from Him, no matter where we might go. He was there when we were being formed in the womb, and His thoughts about us are so numerous that we can't count them. It's humbling just to know that God knows us so well. But David goes even further in verses 23-24, where he says, "Search me, O God, and know my heart; try me, and know my anxieties; and see if there is any wicked way in me, and lead me in the way everlasting."

The first step is complete honesty with God and ourselves. We can start by taking some time alone with God and opening ourselves up to Him. Running from God won't help; it didn't work for Adam and Eve, and it won't work for us. God doesn't want to punish us. Instead He wants to forgive us and give us the grace we need to put the past behind us, live for Him in the present, and trust Him for the future. Our hearts are prepared when we have complete trust in God's mercy and grace.

Written in Our Hearts

A lot of self-help books talk about the benefits of positive affirmations, that is, repeating positive phrases over and over. The word affirmation comes from a Latin word meaning to make firm. As with anything, something that we hear repeatedly makes a strong impression on us; it gets etched in our minds. What we think about continually is written in our hearts, and what is in our hearts controls our lives.

Some might say that they don't believe in affirmations. The only problem with that statement is that it's an affirmation. It may not be positive, but it affirms, or "makes firm," the belief that affirmations don't work. We may not want to believe that repeating positive phrases to ourselves can help, but the fact is that we are constantly affirming what we believe by the things we say. In Matthew 12:34 Jesus says, "... For out of the abundance of the heart the mouth speaks." If we want to know what we really believe, all we have to do is listen to what's coming out of our mouths.

In Joshua 1:8 we read: "This Book of the Law shall not depart from your mouth, but you shall *meditate* in it day and night, that you may observe to do according to all that is written in it. For then you will make your way prosperous, and then you will have good success." The word meditate here means to mutter, or speak, to ourselves. As we speak God's word to ourselves, we repeatedly affirm it, and we literally write it on our hearts.

> *"The eyes of the LORD run to and fro throughout the whole earth, to show Himself strong on behalf of those whose heart is loyal to Him."*
>
> *2 Chronicles 16:9*

Have you ever been sitting in traffic and noticed someone in a car near you having a very animated, maybe even heated, conversation with himself? If he looks over and sees you staring at him, he quickly pretends he was just singing along with the radio or he sheepishly grins and shrugs his shoulders. On occasion we all have those imaginary conversations where we finally tell someone what we really think.

Do we ever wonder how much of our time and emotional energy is simply wasted thinking and talking to ourselves about our problems? It's a waste because most of the conversations we have with ourselves are nothing more then gripe sessions, just one complaint after another. By complaining, we often affirm the negative beliefs in our hearts. We repeatedly talk about what we can't do, or what can't be done, rather than what God can do.

When David went through difficult times, he would write songs and poems about his experiences and remind himself of God's power. Think about what Paul said in Colossians 3:16: "Let the word of Christ dwell in you richly in all wisdom, teaching and admonishing one another in psalms and hymns and spiritual songs, singing with grace in your hearts to the Lord." In other words we have a choice. We can choose to focus our words, and therefore our minds, on God and not the problems. When we're facing difficulties, we can affirm the truth that God is in control and He will make sure that all things work for our ultimate good. Rather than a bunch of negative garbage, we can let God's word live abundantly in our hearts.

At one point David and the men who were fighting with him came to their camp in Ziklag and found that it had been attacked. Everything they had was gone. First Samuel 30:4 says, "Then David and the people who were with him lifted up their voices and wept, until they had no more power to weep." Verse 6 says, "Now David was greatly distressed, for the people spoke of stoning him, because the soul of all the people was grieved, every man for his sons and his daughters. But David strengthened himself in the LORD his God."

It doesn't say exactly how David "strengthened himself," but I imagine that he took time to pray and praise God. Rather than getting more discouraged by talking about the problems, he sang songs and meditated in God's word. While all his men were complaining and looking for someone to blame, David looked to God and found the strength to mount an attack and recover everything that had been taken.

By praying and praising God, we remind ourselves that He is all we need. Just as David did, we pour out our hearts before God, tell Him everything we're feeling, and then remind ourselves that God loves us and He's in control.

When we praise God, remembering all that He's done in the past, it becomes easier to face our current problems. The Bible tells us "the eyes of the LORD run to and fro throughout the whole earth, to show Himself strong on behalf of those whose heart is loyal to Him" (2 Chron. 16:9). As we trust Him, we know that He will continue to help us and to show Himself strong on our behalf.

At a restaurant recently I watched as a four-year-old girl struggled with a big glass of water. She desperately wanted to get a drink on her own, but she just couldn't quite handle it. Her mom held on to the glass with her, and helped her drink without spilling any water.

As parents, we all look forward to the day when our children are independent, when they can support themselves and start to develop a life of their own. But in our relationship with our heavenly Father, He never wants us to become completely independent. It's possible that we could handle a lot of the problems we face without His help, and most people do. Like the little girl, we desperately want to show that we're big enough to do it ourselves. But just dealing with the problems we can handle without God won't help us know God better. It won't give Him a chance to show how much He loves us. And, as David found out, there's so much more that we can accomplish with His help.

Memorizing God's word and spending time meditating on it helps us have His word readily available to us. It's like being able to call a wise friend on the phone when we're feeling down or discouraged. We know we can always count on Him to have the right words to comfort and encourage us. With God's word in our hearts, we will have the faith we need to overcome any challenge that we might face. We'll know that He is able to help us no matter what happens. Our faith will become unshakable, and God will do great things on our behalf.

The Desires of Our Hearts

> "Don't ask what the world needs. Ask what makes you come alive, and go do it. Because what the world needs is people who have come alive."
>
> Howard Thurman

Knowing what we really want, what our hearts' desires are, is important if we want to accomplish much of anything in our lives. In order for us to find fulfillment and joy in what we achieve in life, we have to be sure that our achievements are based on the desires that God has placed in our hearts.

Most of us would like for God to make it easy for us. We think that if God simply told us what we were supposed to do, things would be much simpler. There have been times in my life when I've heard the still small voice of God and had a sense of what God wanted me to do. In some of those times I've thought about Gideon and how he asked God to keep proving to him that he wasn't just imagining the whole thing. I know how Gideon must have felt, because I tend to want something more tangible, like a booming voice out of heaven. I'm sure it would scare me half to death, and I would probably ask God to repeat it on audiotape. But most of the time it just doesn't work that way.

God had already told David that he was going to be the commander over His people. This happened sometime around, or perhaps even before, the story in 1 Samuel 13 when God told Saul that he had taken the kingdom away from him. So, how did God tell David? Like all of us, David probably had to trust that the voice in his head really was God. God's voice is something that we learn to hear over time, by trial and error. It usually comes through a series of events, feelings, and thoughts that the Spirit uses to guide us. It's not an exact science, because it requires that we exercise our faith even if the "facts" seem to be telling us something different.

I think that God must have seen something in David's heart that went beyond simply knowing God and being good at his job. Lots of people do those things, but not many of them are chosen to become king. He must have had some other ambitions. Maybe all the shepherds would stand around the watering hole and complain about the political situation in the land, and perhaps David would listen intently and think about all the things that he'd fix if he could just get the chance.

In some way, David must have been asking God to enlarge his territory, as Jabez prayed in 1 Chronicles 4:10, so that even if God's commandment to become the next king may have taken him by surprise, it wasn't completely out of the blue. David must have felt that he was born to do more than just keep watch over his father's sheep.

Like most people, I've spent a lot of time daydreaming. In *I Could Do Anything — If I Only Knew What it Was*, Barbara Sher talks about the differences between daydreams — what she calls escape dreams — and real dreams. She says, "Escape dreaming is so grand that in a million years you'd never seriously consider doing what you dream about." Real dreams aren't like that. As Barbara puts it, "Where escape dreams are shallow, real dreams are deep and utterly unique to each of us."[1]

Both daydreams and real dreams reveal something about what's in our hearts. They can show us a need that we have, or a desire we want to fulfill. Real dreams touch a chord deep in our hearts, and because they are important to us, we react more emotionally toward them. We might even get a little scared when we think about them. We could be afraid that they will never happen, or maybe even more afraid that they just might come true and change our lives forever.

When we daydream, what do we see ourselves doing? Are there things in our lives that we dream about fixing? Are there adventures we'd like to experience? Are there some talents or skills that we've used on occasion that we'd like to develop further?

CHAPTER 1: *CLARITY*

Howard Thurman said, "Don't ask what the world needs. Ask what makes you come alive, and go do it. Because what the world needs is people who have come alive." What you're looking for are the dreams that resonate deep in your heart, the ones that scare you a little and that make you feel most alive. When you've found them, take some time to write them down. I find that writing about something helps me get a clearer picture of it.

In *Write It Down, Make It Happen*, Henriette Anne Klauser suggests probing even further. In other words, we should go beyond simply putting our dreams into writing and take the time to ask why we want them. How would living those dreams make us feel?

Too often our true desires — the ones that God has given us — get lost in the middle of all the things we think we should be doing with our lives. They get crowded out of our lives when we work hard to make other people happy and when we stop focusing on pleasing God. Trying to get to the bottom of why we want a particular dream can help us uncover what's really in our hearts. When we know what we really want, we're less likely to waste our time doing things that will never fulfill us or please God.

I'm not sure why, but sometimes I've thought that the will of God for my life must be to do something that I hate. I guess it's like taking my medicine; I assume it has to taste bad if it's going to work. But God isn't like that. He created us

> *When we know where we want to go in life, it's a lot easier to avoid things that will take us off track.*

and placed within each of us the desire to learn and do what will bring about His will for our lives.

Beyond fulfilling God's will for our own lives, I'm convinced that every need on earth could be met if each of us would simply do what we most want to do. In other words, if we would follow the desires God has placed in our hearts and use the gifts He's given us, every problem in the world could be solved and we would finally find a deep sense of fulfillment and joy in our work. God knows what the world needs better than we do, and He has provided everything necessary to meet those needs through us.

I learned from David's life that our part might not always be to do some great big work for God. Yes, David became king, but the greatest work that he wanted to do was to build a temple. However, God had other plans. David was able to do all the preparation — even receive the building plans for the temple, but it was his son, Solomon, who actually built it.

There are times when God wants us to be faithful and to prepare the way for someone else. We may not be able to see the completion of the work, but we can find satisfaction in knowing that we did what God wanted from us. Maybe all He wants is for us to plant a seed in someone's life, to give hope to a friend. Whatever the need, God can enable us to meet it, and we will find true satisfaction by fulfilling the desires He places in our hearts.

Many people quote Proverbs 29:18 when they talk about setting goals for their lives. They usually only quote the first half of that verse: "without a vision, people perish" (King James Version). The New King James Version puts it, "The people cast off restraint." A vision or purpose for our lives, whether it's something that God has directly revealed to us or something that is developed out of the desires He has put in our hearts, will help us develop restraint in our lives. It will help us say no to the things that would distract us from God's plan for our lives. When we know where we want to go in life, it's a lot easier to avoid things that will take us off track. We can live with restraint, with more clarity and control, because we know where we're headed.

But what if you're not sure about God's plan for your life? The second half of Proverbs 29:18 says, "But happy is he who keeps the law." We don't have to wait until we have a vision or totally understand God's plan and purpose for our lives. Simply obeying what we see in God's word and doing what we know how to do with the things that are right in front of us will help us create a great life.

Take some time to look at the skills God has given you. What things are easy for you to do? You don't have to be the best in the world. It doesn't matter whether someone is around who seems to be more skilled than you or whether you think you're not all that special. God has the ability to use the skills and talents that we present to Him in the most miraculous ways. When we have a heart to serve people with what we have, God will multiply our talents and abilities.

It will take time and practice for us to become "overnight" successes like David. David's life completely changed in one moment when he defeated Goliath. But it was all the preparation that had gone on in his heart before the battle that actually laid the groundwork for his victory. David had learned to be open and listen to God's voice, even when it meant that he would learn he was wrong and would have to change. He had learned how to find strength through God's word, and he knew what God wanted him to do.

God is working in our lives just like he did in David's. He's preparing us for the work we are uniquely gifted to accomplish. Knowing what God wants to do in our lives can give us the strength and courage to face the challenges we will have along the road to our dreams.

Taking Action

We might think that our prayers have to be perfect or fit some certain pattern if they're going to work. But the most important thing we can do is to simply spend time with God. For example, David complained to God and even questioned what God was doing. But he also always came back to the fact that God was watching over him and taking care of him. Letting God know exactly how we feel, even if it's not always positive, is important. But we do need to be careful that we don't leave those complaints and questions unchallenged by God's truth. As we share our hearts with God, we also need to allow Him to speak to us through His word and remind us that He is taking good care of us. As you spend time in prayer and pour out your heart to Him, also take the time to let Him express His heart to you through His word.

In addition to your normal Bible reading, pick a few verses that really speak to you about some truth you want to see working in your life. Write the verses on a three-by-five-inch index card, then read them out loud to yourself two or three times a day — once in the morning when you get up, then again at midday, and once more right before going to bed. After you read each verse, imagine what things will be like when you experience those truths in your life.

> *Who we are and what's in our hearts control what we do and what we get in life.*

Spend some time writing down the things that you want to achieve. When we look at the goals we want to accomplish, we should think about them in terms of being, doing, and having. In other words, what kind of person do we need to be in order to do and have the things we want in life? Who we are and what's in our hearts control what we do and what we get in life.

Knowing more about ourselves can help us in every area of our lives. One way to learn about ourselves is to take a personality test like the DiSC profile (http://www.onlinedisc.com). Another Web site, http://web.tickle.com/, has a whole series of tests you can take to help determine your personality type, which careers may be a good fit for you, and just about everything else you can imagine. (Note: these tests are not free.)

Many churches have tests you can take to assess your spiritual gifts or talents, and some sites on the Internet offer them as well. These assessments tend to concentrate on the gifts listed in Romans 12:6-8. Check with your pastor to see if your church has them or the DiSC profiles I mentioned above. Also ask friends what gifts they see working in your life. You might be surprised by some of the answers you'll get, so always be sure to spend some time reflecting on the information in prayer. Perhaps others are seeing things you're ignoring.

One simple thing that we can do is to make some lists. Writing down the things we like to do and that we're also good at doing gives us a better idea of the gifts God has given us.

For some it may be easier to write down what they *don't* like instead of what they do like to do. In *The New Psycho-Cybernetics*,[2] I read the story of how Jeff Paul made a list of all the things he did *not* want in a job. He then found a mail-order business that allowed him to avoid all of the things he didn't want to do. He ended up loving what he did and became very successful. He even wrote a book about it called *How To Make $4,000.00 A Day Sitting At Your Kitchen Table In Your Underwear*; which has also become a best-seller.

No matter which lists we make, getting to know our likes and dislikes, our strengths and weaknesses, can help us figure out what to look for in a job or business. The goal is to find something that we will love to do because it will enable us to put all our energy into our work, and that's what will make us successful.

CHAPTER 2

Challenge – Learning to be Faithful

22 TAKING on GOLIATH

Chapter 2

Challenge — Learning to be Faithful

So David rose early in the morning, left the sheep with a keeper, and took the things and went as Jesse had commanded him. And he came to the camp as the army was going out to the fight and shouting for the battle.
~ 1 Samuel 17:20

It had finally reached the point where I just couldn't take it anymore. I found my manager and asked if we could talk. After finding an empty conference room, we sat down and I looked across the table at him and said, "I hate this job."

> "How you do anything, is how you do everything."
>
> T. Harv Eker

The simple fact was that my job wasn't using my experience or abilities, and I was bored and frustrated.

In situations like that, it can be hard to put the proper amount of energy into our work. We often know in our hearts that we're not doing our best, that we're not being faithful with the jobs God has given us.

Some years ago I was working the third shift at a psychiatric hospital. The patients were usually sleeping, so the job wasn't all that demanding and I spent most of the night just sitting around. In some ways that was good, because I was also going to school full-time during the day. But one Sunday a guest speaker came to our church and changed the way I looked at that job and every job I've had since then. He spoke about how important it was to be faithful right where we are.

I realized that no matter what I was doing, no matter where I was, God wanted me to be working for Him. So I decided to stay busy all night, even doing things that I wasn't required to do. I learned that even if the job wasn't the best, I needed to do my best.

God wants me to be faithful and work hard not only because it honors Him and is good for my employer, but also because of what it does for me. As one of my favorite speakers, Jim Rohn, says, "The most important question to ask on the job is not 'What am I getting?' The most important question to ask on the job is 'What am I becoming?'"[1]

It can look like we spend most of our lives doing stuff that doesn't seem all that important in the grand scheme of things. And it's easy to think that it doesn't matter. But as Harv Eker says, "How you do anything, is how you do everything."[2] If I'm unfaithful, undisciplined, and halfhearted in how I approach seemingly unimportant things in my life, even a job that I hate, the chances are good that the same attitude will affect everything else in my life.

Jesus tells us that our faithfulness — or our lack of it — with the small things will determine whether anyone will trust us with bigger responsibilities (Luke 16:10-12).

David Had Been Faithful

I don't know if David had bad days when tending his father's sheep-days when he might have felt frustrated or wanted to quit. I believe that David had big plans for his life and that there may have been times when he wondered if things would ever get better.

What he didn't realize was that running a simple errand for his father, just doing his job, was going to lead to a major change in his life. David's big opportunity came almost completely by surprise.

The Bible doesn't really say, but I imagine that David was very excited when his father asked him to deliver some food to his older brothers. He was going to get an opportunity to see a real battle. The prospect of seeing God's army defeating the Philistines was probably something he was really looking forward to.

As David arrived on the scene, the armies were getting set for battle. The cries went out, and the air was probably full of excitement and fear. For a young man like David, it must have been an incredible experience.

Shortly after David found his brothers, Goliath came out and faced Israel's army. He made the same challenge he had been making for forty days and said: "I defy the armies of Israel this day; give me a man, that we may fight together" (1 Sam. 17:10). Then something happened that I'm sure David hadn't expected. We read that "all the men of Israel, when they saw the man [Goliath], fled from him and were dreadfully afraid" (1 Sam. 17:24).

All of a sudden, the excitement about seeing God's army defeat their enemies was gone. I imagine that David got very angry at Goliath for defying God's army, but he was probably just as angry with the men around him for cowering in fear. How could this happen? Here was God's army running away from a single man. Yes, he was a giant, but he was still just one man.

> God doesn't waste any experience in our lives. No matter what we go through, it all has a purpose.

Unfortunately, Israel had always struggled when it came to battling giants. The generation that came out of Egypt under Moses never saw the Promised Land because they were afraid of fighting the nations and the giants that were there. The Bible tells us that it was their unbelief that condemned them to wander through the wilderness for forty years (Heb. 3:16-19). Rather than believing the truth about what God could do, they chose to believe that the problems were bigger than God (Num. 13).

Old habits and fears tend to die hard, and perhaps part of what bothered David was that history was repeating itself. The entire army was running from an old fear. They had chosen to believe that God couldn't help them.

What they didn't know was that God had been working in a young man's life, preparing him for that very moment. All that David had experienced in his life while working as a lowly shepherd had laid the foundation he needed. David had been faithful in his job, never running from any problem that came his way, and he had used the time and opportunities he'd been given to prepare his heart and hone his skills. The problems he'd overcome while tending sheep had created in him an unshakeable faith in God that was about to change his life forever.

It's possible that David had never seen a battle, let alone fought in one, but that wasn't the important thing. God knew that it wasn't about David or what David thought he could handle. It was about what God was capable of doing through someone who was willing to trust Him.

We tend to say that "God won't give us more than we can handle" when talking about negative events in our lives. But it goes both ways. Just as God's grace and power are available to us when we go through difficult times, they are also there when we face great opportunities. It can be hard to trust God with big problems and opportunities, however, when we haven't trusted Him with our daily struggles.

How do we handle our daily dilemmas — those pesky problems that just keep coming up over and over again? If we run from them, trying hard to ignore them and hoping that they will go away, we waste the very things that God wants to use to prepare us for the opportunities He will present to us later. But when we're faithful, as David was, God can use everything that happens to prepare us for the future. Even little problems that we handle faithfully, and in faith, can become springboards to greater success. Jim Rohn puts it this way: "Don't wish it was easier, wish you were better. Don't wish for less problems, wish for more skills. Don't wish for less challenges, wish for more wisdom."[3]

Seeing His Faithfulness

God doesn't waste any experience in our lives. No matter what we go through, it all has a purpose. Even when it seems like we're stuck and not making any progress at all, we have the opportunity to deepen our relationship with God and strengthen our faith. Learning to recognize His hand at work in the mundane things is harder than seeing it when He's doing big things. But our trust in God — the assurance in our hearts that He will take care of us and work everything for our good — is developed during the daily battles. Facing Goliath would never have been possible for David if he hadn't seen God's power displayed when he was tending sheep.

In Psalm 68:19 David tells us that God "daily loads us with benefits." It's something we need to be reminded of, because we often fail to see God's blessings. Maybe we're too busy to look for them, or perhaps we weren't expecting them. We might assume that God is busy, so we shouldn't bother Him with our little struggles. But expecting God to help us, even in seemingly minor problems, creates situations that God can use to build our faith.

One time several people were struggling with a software problem at work. I had no idea what to do, so I went into the bathroom and prayed. It was a simple prayer: "Lord, man invented computers, and you created man. Surely You can help me figure out what's wrong here." An idea suddenly flashed into my mind, and when I got back to my desk I took a closer look and saw the error. When one of my co-workers complimented me on finding the problem, I told her about my little prayer. She was unimpressed, and I think she even backed up and tried to put a little distance between us. But it was a situation where I clearly saw God answer my prayer by guiding me to a solution.

Have you ever bought a new car and suddenly started seeing cars just like it everywhere? The cars had always been there; you just hadn't been looking for them. But when you own one, they're important to you and you notice them even if you're not specifically looking for them.

It's the same with God's blessings. They're all around us, showing us that He is there and that He is faithful, but we don't see them because they're not important for us and we're not looking for them. If we think that God only gets involved with the major things in our lives and we don't see the importance of recognizing His daily benefits, we miss learning about His faithfulness.

> *Circumstances happen to all of us but it's how we react to them that determines their effect on us.*

One of the reasons I think prayer, praise, and worship are so important is that through them we remind ourselves that we depend on God and that He is faithful. By deciding to bring every need — no matter how small — to God and then consciously seeking His blessings, we increase the importance we place on those blessings. The more important they become, the more we will see them. The more we see them, the stronger our faith will become. As our faith in God grows, He will be able to do more in our lives. It's a never-ending cycle that will open our eyes to see how God can help us in every situation, with every problem, and in every opportunity that will come our way.

Circumstance or Challenge?

A couple of years ago I read about a man who was suing his local cable TV provider. In the lawsuit, he alleged that his wife and children were fat, lazy, and unmotivated and that it was the cable company's fault. He claimed that he had canceled his subscription, but that the company had continued to provide them with cable TV. Because the service hadn't been canceled, they had spent way too much time in front of the tube, causing major problems for his family. I don't know what happened with this ridiculous lawsuit, but I hope it was thrown out of court.

When dealing with life's problems we have a couple of choices. We can decide whether we want to be victors or victims. We can choose to overcome life's challenges or succumb to our circumstances. For the man in this story, it seems that the circumstance of having cable TV was too much to handle. The sad thing is that many people feel the same way about things in their lives. They believe that everything happens to them and that there is nothing they can do about it. They see themselves as helpless victims of circumstance.

In John 16:33, Jesus tells us, "These things I have spoken to you, that in Me you may have peace. In the world you will have tribulation; but be of good cheer, I have overcome the world." In other words, things will happen to us that we can't control. But as Romans 8:37 tells us, "Yet in all these things we are more than conquerors through Him who loved us." We can conquer and overcome *in* the tribulations because Christ overcame. Our personal limitations don't matter because we can experience God's power in the midst of our circumstances.

Circumstances happen to all of us but it's how we react to them that determines their effect on us. For some people, the loss of a job begins a downward spiral into hopelessness and despair. For others, losing a job becomes the best thing that ever happened to them, positively affecting their lives in countless ways. Some people who suffer a tragedy become angry and bitter, while others emerge from similar tragedies with renewed hope and faith. It's not what happens to us that matters, but whether or not we look to God in our struggles.

While thousands of soldiers cowered before Goliath and believed that he was unbeatable, David saw an opportunity for God to show Himself strong. Rather than look at the circumstances, David chose to look at God. When everyone else was focused on their weaknesses, David decided to concentrate on God's power. The circumstances were the same for all of them, but David was the only one who was able to see this as a great opportunity for God to work a miracle.

In 2 Kings 6 we read about the king of Syria sending troops to capture the prophet Elisha. Syria and Israel were at war, and every time the king of Syria came up with a battle plan, God would tell Elisha about it and Elisha would tell the king of Israel. The Syrian king was angry because he thought that one of his men was helping the king of Israel. His men told him that it was Elisha the prophet who was revealing his secret plans. The king then decided to capture Elisha, so he sent a great army that arrived during the night and surrounded the city where Elisha was staying.

In the morning, Elisha's servant woke up and saw that the Syrian army had surrounded them. In 2 Kings 6:15 the servant says to Elisha, "Alas, my master! What shall we do?" In verses 16-17 we read, "So he answered, 'Do not fear, for those who are with us are more than those who are with them.' And Elisha prayed, and said, 'LORD, I pray, open his eyes that he may see.' Then the LORD opened the eyes of the young man, and he saw. And behold, the mountain was full of horses and chariots of fire all around Elisha."

The goal isn't to be perfect in what we do but to learn to trust God in all that we do.

When we go through tribulations it can be good to do what Elisha did for his servant. We can pray that God will open our eyes so that we'll see that we are not powerless in the face of our circumstances but that God has given us all that we need in order to overcome them. With our natural eyes we will only see the problems that everyone else sees, so we need God's help to be able to look at things through His eyes. There are no circumstances we will face that God can't change or give us the grace to handle.

We experience success throughout our lives because we've been faithful, looking to and trusting in God through all the daily struggles. Our faith in God is strong when big opportunities come, because the little victories we've experienced with God have taught us that we can trust Him. As our responsibilities and opportunities grow, we can have confidence in God's power and grace to meet every new challenge.

Taking Action

Learning to trust God and to see Him working in our lives starts with becoming aware of the areas where we need His help. We need help in every area, and it's good to take some time to sit down and put a list together. How faithful are we in our personal and spiritual lives? How about the relationships we have with our spouses, children, family, and friends? What specific things can we improve in our careers? How about finances? What can we do to be more faithful with our physical, mental, and emotional health?

The goal isn't to be perfect in what we do but to learn to trust God in all that we do. Becoming more aware of the areas where we need God and letting Him work in our lives in those areas, will give us a chance to see God's faithfulness. Bringing these areas to God in prayer, and seeking His help, will not only improve our faithfulness in them, but it will also strengthen our faith in Him.

CHAPTER 3

Consequences — Risks and Rewards

Chapter 3

Consequences — Risks and Rewards

Then David spoke to the men who stood by him, saying, "What shall be done for the man who kills this Philistine and takes away the reproach from Israel? For who is this uncircumcised Philistine, that he should defy the armies of the living God?" ~ 1 Samuel 17:26

Could you possibly win if you couldn't lose? That question has always been on my mind since I heard Jim Rohn ask it five years ago. I had the chance to see Jim at a live event and even to have lunch with him (and thirty other people) in St. Louis, Missouri. It was a wonderful time that I will always remember. The notes that I wrote that day, which Jim signed for me, are still in the front of my journal.

Even though we don't like risk, the question we have to ask is: Could we succeed if we couldn't fail? Would success have any meaning at all if there was no such thing as failure? It doesn't seem possible to have the one without the other. These "opposites in conflict," as Jim put it that day in St. Louis, are what create the adventure we call life.

The conflict of opposites also seems to imply that there will always be a battle. Even when we've reached some level of success, constant vigilance is required to maintain it. Proverbs 27:23-24 says, "Be diligent to know the state of your flocks, and attend to your herds; for riches are not forever, nor does a crown endure to all generations." It may be discouraging to hear that success doesn't last, but neither does failure. Whether we succeed or fail, it's important to remember that it's just a temporary event.

I've always wanted a lush, green lawn. The problem is that I've never liked doing yard work. I sometimes picture myself as the man in the parable of the tares and wheat from Matthew 13. I wake up one morning to find that someone has sown crabgrass and dandelions in my yard, and I decide simply to let them grow together with the grass. The difference between the man in the parable and me is that I'm never going to separate the weeds from the grass because that would take too much time and work.

> *While we spend a lot of time thinking about the process and the price, most of us lose sight of the goal we will reach or the dream we will realize, and we forget about the prize.*

One thing I've learned by watching my neighbors is that the only way to have a nice lawn is to work at it constantly, all summer long. The weeds are always lurking in the ground waiting for the opportunity to take control. It goes all the way back to the fall of man in Genesis. No matter how we feel about it, if we want to grow something special, we not only have to plant the right kind of seed, but we also have to fight against everything else. The ground, and life for that matter, will always yield "thorns and thistles" (Gen. 3:18) unless we're willing to work and create something better.

Chapter 3: CONSEQUENCES

Perhaps we should be wary if someone offers us the "secret to permanent success." The truth seems to be that there will always be a battle to get what we want and an ongoing struggle to keep it. Whether it's in our relationships, finances, health, or any other area of our lives, bad things come up if we just sit back and wait to see what happens. One of the facts of life is that nothing stands still. We're either moving forward or losing ground.

The fact that risk and work are involved keeps most people from even attempting to accomplish their goals or fulfill their dreams. The problem is that the difficulties and struggles will always be there whether we choose to get by with a little or whether we work hard for what we want. Since there is no easy street and we're going to have to work for whatever we get in life, why not work to have what we really want rather than what grows by itself?

The Process, the Price, and the Prize

Whatever we want to achieve in life will involve going through some sort of process; in other words, there will be things that we need to learn and do. Sometimes the only way to learn is by actually trying, making mistakes, learning from those mistakes, and starting over again.

The process can take a long time, and there's no way around it. In order to have things in life we've never had before, we need to do things we've never done before. This means learning new things, and becoming the kind of person who will persistently work toward our goals.

Whatever it costs us in time, energy, and emotions to go through the process is the price we have to pay to achieve what we want. Everything has its price, whether it's working when you'd rather be relaxing or having to hear a few dozen people say "no" for every "yes" that you get. The thing that stops most people from reaching their dreams is the perception that the price will be too high — that it will cost them more, particularly in terms of the emotional investment, than they are willing to pay.

While we spend a lot of time thinking about the process and the price, most of us lose sight of the goal we will reach or the dream we will realize, and we forget about the prize. We can have whatever we want in life if we know what it is and if we're willing to pay the price to get it. Whatever it may be, we have to ask ourselves about every dream: "Am I willing to pay the price and go through the process?" If the answer is no, then we may have to set our sights lower and dream smaller dreams.

The one cost that most of us don't figure into our calculations is the price of not achieving our dreams. What will it cost us to stay at that job we hate? What will we lose if we give our lives to something that has never ignited our passions? In other words, are we willing to settle for a life that will never live up to our expectations of what we could have achieved? How will we feel at the end of our lives when we look back with regret at all we never even attempted?

When looking at the price, we often have misconceptions about what we will have to do in order to get the prize we want. Many believe that the only way to be successful in one area of their lives is to make sacrifices in all the others. But

Chapter 3: CONSEQUENCES

let me be clear about one thing: I don't believe that you have to sacrifice your family, friends, or health in order to be successful. Unfortunately, later in David's life, he didn't give his family the kind of attention that it needed. He ended up paying a very high price — one that could have been avoided.

I believe that it's possible to be successful in every area of our lives. If someone is only successful in the career and financial areas, then he's not really all that successful. Being successful isn't a matter of "either/or." For example, some people might think that they can either be successful or have a happy family. True success is having both, and that should always be our goal.

When looking at the process, price, and prize, we may have to realize that in order to have it all, the process could take a long time or that the price of having it all means we have to be less self-centered with our downtime. Whatever it may be, once we know what we want (the prize), it's just a matter of determining what we have to learn and do (the process) and deciding to pay the price.

Knowing the Prize is Right

There's an old story about a man who went into a small country store and noticed a dog whimpering in the corner. He asked the storeowner if it was his dog. "Yes, it is," the owner said. "Why is your dog whimpering like that?" he asked. "Oh, he's lying on a nail," the owner answered. The

> **Taking the time to know what we value and what's most important to us about reaching our dreams can help ensure that we don't spend our lives pursuing the wrong things.**

man asked, "Then why doesn't he just get up?" The owner replied, "I guess it just doesn't hurt bad enough."

There are times when the only way to get moving toward our dreams is actually to increase the pain that is caused by the difference between where we are now and where we want to be, because we always have to deal with the problem of inertia. Inertia is the tendency for things to stay as they are. If we're not moving toward our dreams, inertia will keep us from reaching them because it will hold us right where we are. We have to look within ourselves to find the motivation to stop complaining about the nail and to actually get up off of it.

We read in 1 Samuel 17:25 that when David first heard Goliath's challenge, he also overheard the soldiers around him talking about the rewards the king would give to the man who defeated Goliath. David even asked a couple of different people exactly what the rewards were going to be. It was an impressive list. The king was offering to make the person who killed Goliath wealthy, give his family freedom from taxation, and allow him to marry his daughter. Defeating Goliath was going to bring fame and fortune to David and his family.

There are times when we do things for reasons that aren't always clear to everyone else. It's possible that David fought Goliath because of the rewards he would receive from the king. But was there something else that drove him? Maybe he was just really angry at Goliath's defiance of God's army, or perhaps he saw this battle as an opportunity to take a big step toward fulfilling his dream of becoming king. The story in 1 Samuel 17 doesn't really say. But whatever the prize may have been that David wanted, it must have been very compelling because he was willing to risk everything in order to have it.

The prizes that we work for in our lives fall into one of two main categories: the external benefits we can receive like fame and fortune and the internal benefits such as a sense of accomplishment and knowing that we've done something that was right in terms of our values or fulfilling the desires of our hearts. We have to be careful that we aren't chasing after the external benefits alone, and we need to be sure that reaching our prizes will give us a sense of pride not only in what we've done but also in the people that we've become in the process.

It's unfortunate when people sacrifice their family, friends, health, or integrity in the pursuit of some prize only to find out that it was the wrong thing. In the end, it didn't meet their deepest needs or fulfill the true desires of their heart. They paid too high a price for the wrong prize.

Taking the time to know what we value and what's most important to us about reaching our dreams can help ensure that we don't spend our lives pursuing the wrong things. Our goal should always be to fulfill the true desires of our hearts — the things that really make us tick. It's not about what other people want us to do. God has specifically gifted us and placed desires in our hearts so that He can accomplish His will through us.

What Are the Risks?

Zig Ziglar talks about the confidence that accompanies ignorance. There are times when not knowing what's at stake may mean we're not afraid. We might even believe that if we just don't think about what could go wrong, there will be nothing to fear. But things do go wrong, and it's better to be clear about the risks before we start something and to do all we can either to avoid problems or to lessen their potential impact. At the same time, we shouldn't let the potential risks cause us to become so afraid that we don't act.

Proverbs 22:3 says, "A prudent man foresees evil and hides himself, but the simple pass on and are punished." Being prudent, or wise, means being able to properly assess risks and rewards, take steps to avoid possible problems, and move forward intelligently and confidently. We're not confident because we don't know any better; we are confident because we understand that we're doing the best we can.

I tend to be very analytical. I tell people that I want to be sure I'm doing the right thing, but I know in my heart that sometimes I'm just making excuses. It can be too easy to overanalyze everything, constantly asking "what if" questions. What if things don't work out? What if I'm wrong? What if I don't have the skills? What if . . . what if? It can become a seemingly endless litany of problems with very few solutions.

> *But rather than focusing on all that could go wrong, he chose to place his attention on the outcome that he wanted.*

Ironically, I used to get really frustrated at work when we'd get stuck in meetings where the whole conversation revolved around endless "what ifs." We'd spend hours trying to determine everything that could go wrong and make one plan after another for dealing with the problems, should they arise.

The really frustrating part was that if anything did go wrong, we would call emergency meetings and try to figure out what we were going to do. Sometimes we simply forgot what we'd talked about at the previous meetings or we all remembered something different. There were times when we realized our best-laid plans wouldn't have worked anyway. Hours and hours, maybe even days' or weeks' worth of time, were wasted worrying about potential problems that never happened and making contingency plans on top of contingency plans, none of which ever got used.

The potential risk for David was huge. If he lost, not only would he be dead, but many other people would die as well and the nation of Israel would be enslaved. It's only a guess, but I have to assume that David fully understood the risks involved. However, he was convinced he had to fight Goliath, and he knew beyond any doubt that God would win the battle for him.

Focus on the Desired Outcome

We don't really know what went on in David's mind as he looked at the whole situation. But rather than focusing on all that could go wrong, he chose to place his attention on the outcome that he wanted. He didn't really know how he would do it; he just knew that he had to win.

Looking at 1 Samuel 17:45-47, we see that David had put together a fairly detailed picture of the outcome he wanted. He saw God delivering Goliath into his hands and himself killing Goliath and cutting off his head. He even saw the birds and wild beasts eating the dead carcasses of the Philistine army. It was a pretty gruesome picture, but David made sure he had a clear and detailed picture in his mind before he walked out to face Goliath.

When we start thinking about taking steps toward our dreams, it's easy to imagine that we will face difficulties. Often they're just vague images of problems and potential failure. When we focus on the outcome we want, it's important to make the picture as clear as possible. The positive image of the outcome we want needs to be stronger in our minds than the negative images we have about going through the process and paying the price.

The power of mental images is demonstrated by what happens to us when we watch movies. For example, my wife refuses to watch movies about submarines because they make her feel claustrophobic. I've tried to explain to her that the movie was filmed on a set; it's not a real submarine, and they're not really underwater. But it doesn't seem to make any difference. Most people have similar experiences — they get emotionally involved in a movie and almost feel like they're part of it. It's a proven fact that the subconscious mind can't tell the difference between a vividly imagined experience and a real one. That's why we get scared or angry, laugh, or cry when we watch a movie, even when we know that it's just a movie.

One technique that can help us to focus on our desired outcome is to create our own movie. In this movie we see ourselves accomplishing our goal. We imagine the sights, sounds, and even the smells that we will experience after reaching our goal. As we watch the mental movie we should experience the emotions we'd like to have associated with reaching our goal. Emotion is a powerful motivator. Positive emotions can help us want to do something, and negative emotions motivate us to avoid it. Having strong, positive emotions while watching the movie of our success will help us focus on the outcome we want. The more vivid we make the movie and the more often we watch it, the easier it will be to stay on track toward our goal.

Too often we concentrate on the process and the price and spend very little time thinking about the prize. Because we know that we'll have difficulties and setbacks, we might decide it's not worth it. We feel it's not worth it only because we haven't really taken the time to get a clear picture of the prize. The struggles we imagine facing are unclear, but because they are more immediate, they occupy our minds more than the future benefits which are hazy and too far away. We give up before we even start because we don't take the time to get the whole picture. When we know exactly what we'll gain — when we're sure of the prize — going through the process and paying the price will be easier and well worth the effort.

Taking Action

Look at the goals you wrote down as part of the action steps from chapter 1 on clarity. For each of the goals take some time to consider the process by asking

But also ask this: What will I lose if I don't take action on this dream?

yourself questions like: What obstacles do I have to overcome? What information, training, or skills do I need? Who can help me accomplish this goal?

Some questions to help you think about the price involved are: What will I need to sacrifice — watching TV, a hobby, etc. — in order to find the time to work on my goal? What expenses can I reduce, or eliminate, so that I will have the money I need to help me reach my goal?

One word of caution: The price doesn't have to involve quitting your job. Before taking such a drastic step, make sure that you are doing all you can to eliminate everything that is unnecessary in your life. A lot of our time and money are often wasted doing things that don't help us move toward our goals. Making sure that we take advantage of all the time and money we currently have is good stewardship, and it should always be the first step. Budgeting our time is even more important than budgeting our money, because time is our most valuable resource. While it's possible to make more money, no one can make more time.

When looking at your goals, think about the benefits you'll gain from reaching them, that is, the prize. Ask some questions like: What will I gain from accomplishing this dream? How will accomplishing this goal make me feel? How will reaching this goal benefit my family and those closest to me?

But also ask this: What will I lose if I don't take action on this dream? Most people are more motivated by the fear of loss than they are by the desire for gain. It's much too easy to decide we don't want to make the sacrifices involved if we're not clear about the benefits we'll lose by not pursuing our dreams.

In Luke 11:9-10, Jesus said, "So I say to you, ask, and it will be given to you; seek, and you will find; knock, and it will be opened to you. For everyone who asks receives, and he who seeks finds, and to him who knocks it will be opened." God will ensure that all the information and help we need will come our way. All we have to do is ask, seek, and knock. Problems are bound to arise as we follow our dreams, but as we confidently trust in God's supply, we'll find that He is preparing the way before us. Work (the process) and sacrifice (the price) will still be involved, but we will also reap the rewards (the prize) as God blesses us abundantly.

CHAPTER 4

Confrontation — Handling Criticism

Chapter 4

Confrontation — Handling Criticism

Now Eliab his oldest brother heard when he spoke to the men; and Eliab's anger was aroused against David, and he said, "Why did you come down here? And with whom have you left those few sheep in the wilderness? I know your pride and the insolence of your heart, for you have come down to see the battle." ~ 1 Samuel 17:28

As I watched people put money in a slot machine at the airport in Las Vegas, it occurred to me that most people see success as something that happens by chance. They feel that the only way they will be able to improve their lives is if Lady Luck smiles on them and they win a lot of money. They look with envy and suspicion at people who have become successful because they assume that those people must have had some unfair advantage.

We learned early in life that fitting in is better than standing out.

When we embark on our journey toward success, we hope that the people who love us will encourage and support us. Sadly, that's not always what happens. Sometimes our family and closest friends try to talk us out of our plans. They have lots of good reasons, and they can also be very convincing.

Unfortunately, some people aren't interested in seeing "one of their own" make good because it sheds some unwanted light on their own lives. Many people choose to complain about life rather than do something about it. They may not have chosen the circumstances they're in, but they wake up every day and decide to stay in the same old rut. As long as all their friends stay in the rut with them, they will never have to face the fact that things can and do change.

You might hear people say, "I know a guy who knew a guy whose uncle's friend had an acquaintance who tried that, and it didn't work." It's rare that they can speak from personal experience, and all too frequently the "advice" is negative and discouraging. They may mean well, but it's likely that they haven't taken many big chances or had much success in their own lives, so there isn't much that they can tell us that will help. We need to learn to be understanding and forgiving, yet not let them talk us out of pursuing our dreams.

Then there are people like Eliab, David's brother, who go beyond negative and discouraging all the way to demeaning and belittling. Mark Twain's advice for dealing with people like that is, "Keep away from people who try to belittle your ambitions. Small people always do that, but the really great make you feel that you, too, can become great."[1]

As children we found out that being different could be unpleasant. Kids don't know how to deal with someone who thinks and acts differently. The typical response was to be mean and hurtful, so we learned early in life that fitting in is better than standing out. As long as we were just like all the other kids, the other kids would like us. A constant concern from then on was: "What does So-and-So think of me?"

CHAPTER 4: CONFRONTATION

In Arthur Miller's play *The Death of a Salesman*, Willy Loman, the main character, says, "The goal in life is to be liked." Earl Nightingale points out in his audio program *Lead the Field* that Willy never grew up. He was stuck thinking like a child, where gaining the approval of others was more important than expressing his uniqueness.

The people we spend most of our time with have a profound impact on our lives. We tend to think and act like they do. Even when we become adults, it's hard to risk losing the approval of those around us and doing something that none of them has ever done. The result is usually mediocrity, or worse. Because God has uniquely gifted each of us and placed within our hearts the desire to express those gifts, people who spend their lives doing what *others* think they should do will always be unhappy. If they continue to seek the approval of their peers and not God, they end up frustrated and miserable. Even if they make a good living, they never really enjoy life or become truly successful.

Most people would probably agree with the masses in Las Vegas that success is a matter of luck and timing. They don't believe that there is a clear process for success or that we have the ability to make significant changes in our lives simply by changing our thinking and making new choices. In one conversation after another, people repeat the same old excuses and reasons why "people like us" can't

> **The single most important factor that contributed to a person's career success, with all other factors being equal, was his "reference group."**

get ahead. Rather than challenging and encouraging each other to have more faith, take more chances and do more with our lives, they continually reinforce the belief that it's just too hard and there's nothing they can do about it. No one dares to ask if that belief is true, because so many people are convinced that it is. And when the Bible says, "all things are possible to him who believes" (Mark 9:23), almost everyone thinks, "Well . . . yeah, but. . . ."

Who's Influencing Whom?

In his article on "Building Your Network,"[2] Brian Tracy describes a twenty-five-year study done at Harvard University in which Dr. David McLelland found that the single most important factor that contributed to a person's career success, with all other factors being equal, was his "reference group." A person's reference group is the people with whom he spends most of his time and with whom he identifies.

Proverbs 22:24-25 warns us not to associate with an angry person because we may learn his ways. Proverbs 12:26 tells us that the wicked can lead the righteous astray, and I Corinthians 15:33 says that bad associations ruin good habits.

It's not all negative, however, because there is also the positive side of spending time with people. Hebrews 10:25 encourages believers to spend time together so that we can exhort and comfort each other, especially as the day of Jesus' return approaches.

Most of us don't want to hang out with or be associated with really bad people, but the issue goes beyond that to

Chapter 4: CONFRONTATION

all of our associations. All people express what they believe through their words and actions. As we spend time with people, what they say and do will influence our thinking and thereby our beliefs. This becomes a cycle because what we think and talk about influences our beliefs, and then those beliefs further influence what we think and talk about. Since our thoughts control how we feel and act, ultimately they affect the results we get in life. The reason our reference group is such a powerful factor in determining our success is because that group is influencing what we believe and how we think and act.

A couple of years ago we were with a church group when a woman in the group slipped and hurt her ankle. Everyone quickly gathered and offered up prayers of faith for her healing. As soon as the prayers ended, several people felt they had to share their own personal horror stories about accidents and broken bones. I'm sure most of them meant well, but I began to wonder why we'd spent time praying for healing. Our faith certainly wasn't helped, and it was probably severely hampered, by the ensuing conversation.

I don't believe we have to maintain a positive "confession" while trying to ignore the facts. It's like the joke about three religious people who end up in hell. One of them says, "In the church I attended, we didn't believe in hell. I can't believe I'm here!" The second one moans and says, "In my church, we believed that once you were a member of the church, you were guaranteed a spot in heaven. I don't believe this is happening!" The third member of this unhappy group replies, "I know where I am, but I'm not confessing it."

Ignoring problems in the hope that they will go away or that it will bolster our sagging faith isn't the answer. As I mentioned earlier, we need to understand the risks and problems that we could face as we pursue our dreams. We stand in faith not because we refuse to acknowledge the problems, but because we know that God is greater than those problems. As Michael Beckwith says, "Don't take your big problems to God; take a big God to your problems."

Part of our problem is caused by not believing in a real God who loves us and who wants to bless us. Hebrews 11:6 tells us that "without faith it is impossible to please Him, for he who comes to God must believe that He is, and that He is a rewarder of those who diligently seek Him." Our lives should be living examples of the kind of faith that shows in our actions and says "I believe that an all-powerful, loving God exists, and I will seek Him because I know that He wants to do great things in my life."

As we look at our own reference groups, some questions we should ask ourselves are: How have our past associations, family, and friends influenced our beliefs and our lives up to this point? Are the conversations we have with our friends helping, or hurting, our faith? What can we learn about our own beliefs and ourselves by examining the people with whom we spend our time? Why do we spend time with them? What need are they meeting in our lives?

As one person put it, if you're the smartest person in your group, you need a new group. Jim Rohn recommends that we stay away from the easy crowd. The easy crowd will help us feel comfortable with who we are and encourage us to stay right where we are in life. Their goal is to maintain the status quo. The reason we feel comfortable around them is because they don't challenge us. In order to grow, we need to start spending time with people who want more from life — with a crowd that will challenge and help us become more than we are today.

I don't know if David's family encouraged him as he was growing up. From things that we read about later in his life, we know that he learned to find strength in God in spite of how everyone else around him was feeling. When he struggled with difficulties and trials, he was able to pour out his concerns and his complaints to God and rededicate himself to trusting God. In spite of the negative comments from his brother, David held to the conviction that God was going to make him victorious. He maintained an attitude of positive faith in the face of opposition.

> **When they criticize us, we should recognize that they're just stating their opinions, and we have a choice.**

Even if David hadn't had the best environment growing up, he had learned how to overcome the fear of failure and the fear of all that might possibly go wrong with faith in what God could do. He knew that he didn't have to think like everyone else. David seems to have developed one very important trait that every good leader possesses, in tough times he could inspire hope and courage in those who followed him. When everyone else was talking about failure, David maintained his faith in God.

Finding Diamonds in the Rough

I took German in high school and spent a summer in Germany between my junior and senior years. It was during that summer that I developed a desire to live and work in Germany. But after becoming a Christian, getting married, and having kids, it didn't seem likely that I'd ever get to live there. In 1983, God spoke to me about going to Germany in three to four years' time.

I have to admit, it was quite a shock to my wife. Fortunately, God in His faithfulness had already been at work in her life; she had also taken German in high school.

We immediately began working with our pastor and doing all we could to prepare for the move to Germany. After two years of preparation, the leadership in our church changed. Another pastor took over the reins, and I started meeting with him to continue getting ready for our move. For reasons that I never totally understood, he and I never saw eye to eye. It seemed there was a clash of personalities and too many differences of opinion. On top of that, the new pastor had no interest in foreign missions.

My original vision for Germany had been to move to Stuttgart and start a church. The new pastor was quick to point out that I was a teacher, not a pastor, and "teachers don't start churches." At the time, this was extremely discouraging, but I held on to my vision for Germany and prayed that God would work out all the details.

In 1986, three and a half years after God had spoken to me about going to Germany, God opened the doors for me

Chapter 4: CONFRONTATION

to transfer to Munich. I knew it was His leading, so I agreed to take the job. Upon hearing the news, our pastor was less than enthused. He was very critical of the "bad decision" I had made. He agreed to bless us as we went, but told us he would not support the work we wanted to do in Germany.

When facing criticism, we have to realize that everybody has his own view of things. Everyone else's viewpoint is going to be different from ours, and that's OK. I'm sure that as David walked out on the field of battle against Goliath, there were soldiers scratching their heads and asking themselves if Saul had lost his mind. They were probably convinced that David was incapable of beating Goliath. After all, he was a shepherd boy, not a soldier, and shepherd boys don't kill giants.

One of my mentors, Les Brown, talks about something a teacher once told him: "Other people's opinions of you don't have to become your reality." People have their opinions and their beliefs. What they believe about us isn't necessarily right or wrong, true or false; it's simply their belief. When they criticize us, we should recognize that they're just stating their opinions, and we have a choice. We can accept or reject parts of it or all of it.

When we receive criticism or advice, it's important that we separate what's true from what isn't true. For example, if I look at what my pastor said to me and ask myself if it's true that I am a teacher and not a pastor, the answer would be that it's definitely true. Most pastors like to do one-on-one counseling and shepherding. I tend to find that preaching and teaching in front of groups is a lot easier for me. So, given my general understanding of the difference between a teacher and a pastor, I am definitely a teacher.

Is it true that teachers can't start churches? If I were faced with a similar situation today, I'd have to say that statement isn't true. I'm sure I could find several examples of people whose primary gifting was teaching but who had successfully started churches. Our pastor was stating something as a fact that really was nothing more than his opinion: only pastors can start churches.

> *The very counsel that God may be trying to use to help us refine our vision and to put us on the right course can feel like a blow to the gut.*

As I mentioned, there seemed to be a clash of personalities that fueled some of the problems I had with this pastor. It's easy to disregard what someone says when you know that they don't like you or that they're just saying something out of spite. But we need to learn how to find the hidden blessing in every criticism. Had I tried to find the blessing, the diamond in the rough, I would have realized that perhaps I was being given a key piece of information.

I had based my vision for Germany on a faulty assumption — the assumption that starting a church was the only reason for going to a foreign country. I had assumed that all missionaries were church builders, and that's not entirely true. Missionaries do a lot of different things. Once we were in Germany, we found that there was a vital need for teaching within the existing churches. There were a lot of opportunities to use our gifts, and none of them involved starting a church. We saw God do some wonderful things as He touched people through our ministry while we simply endeavored to support the local church.

Saul was quick to point out to David, "You are not able to go against this Philistine to fight with him; for you are a youth, and he a man of war from his youth." (1 Sam. 17:33) Saul was a seasoned warrior, and he knew what he was talking about. In other words, there was a lot of truth in Saul's criticism. David wasn't a man of war, but Goliath was. David couldn't hope to win this battle by fighting Goliath on Goliath's terms. Saul's criticism became a key piece of information. David needed to look at what he did well and to rely on his own strengths. In other words, he needed to do what he did best, and using a sword and shield would have been a major mistake.

When someone tells us that our plans stink, it can be easy to get discouraged and feel sorry for ourselves. The very counsel that God may be trying to use to help us refine our vision and to put us on the right course can feel like a blow to the gut. David didn't ignore Saul's opinion, but he also didn't let it discourage him. Instead of saying, "Oh well, I guess this wasn't such a good idea after all" or "You're right, I'm the wrong person for this job; I guess I'll just go home," David held firmly to the belief that God was going to give him victory.

Even though Saul may have been trying to discourage David, David looked at his statements as good advice. Proverbs 20:18 puts it this way: "Plans are established by counsel; by wise counsel wage war." None of us has all the answers. There are times when the counsel we need will come from people who are trying to talk us out of our plans. Learning to listen to what is being said and not taking it personally can actually save us a lot of trouble.

Occasionally we need to be able to put some emotional distance between us and the criticism we receive. The criticism may hurt at first, temporarily taking the wind out of our sails. Recognizing it as someone's opinion, separating truth from untruth, and looking for the blessings can help us take even the harshest criticism from our worst critic and turn it into some of the best advice we've ever been given. David did that, and look at what he was able to do.

Taking Action

This is another time when using a pen and paper will be very helpful. Think about some of the criticism that you've received throughout your life, particularly that which has been the most discouraging. As you think about the criticism, remember that it was just someone's opinion, then ask the following questions: What is true about what he said? What isn't true? Where is the blessing in this criticism?

Make a habit of doing this every time someone shares "advice" with you. You will come to realize that God can speak to you through a variety of people, and in a lot of different ways. Numbers 22 tells about a man named Balaam. God had to open the mouth of his donkey in order for him to realize that he was making a mistake. I've

Chapter 4: Confrontation

always found it interesting that Balaam got so angry about what had happened and about his plans getting messed up that he actually started arguing with his donkey. I guess Balaam was a slow learner.

We can always hope that we don't get so set in our ways that God has to open the mouths of our dogs or cats in order to get our attention. Regardless of where the advice ends up coming from, being open to advice and counsel — even correction if need be — can mean the difference between success and failure.

Take a good look at your reference group. What do the people you spend your time with have you thinking, saying, and doing? You may find that there are people in your life who are costing you too much, both emotionally and financially. Unfortunately, some people cause more harm than good. You may need to limit the amount of time you spend with them or the amount of influence they have over you. In some cases you may even need to end the relationship.

Jesus tells us, "Assuredly, I say to you, there is no one who has left house or brothers or sisters or father or mother or wife or children or lands, for My sake and the gospel's, who shall not receive a hundredfold now in this time — houses and brothers and sisters and mothers and children and lands, with persecutions — and in the age to come, eternal life" (Mark

> *We can always hope that we don't get so set in our ways that God has to open the mouth of our dog or cat in order to get our attention.*

10:29-30). As difficult as the choice may be, we know that God will help us meet like-minded people who will help and support us in this life and that we will receive eternal blessings as well.

CHAPTER 5

Confidence — Learning to Trust

CHAPTER 5

Confidence — Learning to Trust

But David said to Saul, "Your servant used to keep his father's sheep, and when a lion or a bear came and took a lamb out of the flock, I went out after it and struck it, and delivered the lamb from its mouth; and when it arose against me, I caught it by its beard, and struck and killed it. Your servant has killed both lion and bear; and this uncircumcised Philistine will be like one of them, seeing he has defied the armies of the living God." Moreover David said, "The LORD, who delivered me from the paw of the lion and from the paw of the bear, He will deliver me from the hand of this Philistine." ~ 1 Samuel 17:34-37

When my wife and I made the decision to move to Germany in 1983, we did some things that really helped us prepare. We put a map of Germany on the dining room wall where we would constantly see it. We were able to get some tapes of German praise and worship music, which we listened to all the time. After a little searching we found a couple of German tutors, so my wife and I both started taking weekly lessons. We put together a prayer list and began interceding on behalf of the Germans and Germany. We even met an elderly German woman whom we visited several times a month. She enjoyed having some company, and it was a good opportunity for us to speak German.

Even though we didn't know what we were doing at the time, we couldn't have put together a better plan for our preparation. Not only were we sharpening our language skills and learning about the culture, but looking at that map every day was keeping the vision fresh in our minds.

There were occasions during our three- to four-year preparation when I got anxious. I wondered if God was really going to open the doors for us to move to Germany. Almost exactly three and a half years after I felt God speak to me, I was able to see a long-standing dream of mine fulfilled. Through a series of events where I could clearly see God's hand at work, He opened the door for us to move to Germany, and the company I was working for was footing the bill! It was win-win, because they needed my expertise and I couldn't have afforded to live there any other way. Proverbs 13:12 tells us, "Hope deferred makes the heart sick, but when the desire comes, it is a tree of life."

> *He does greater things than we could have imagined, because when we recognize that we can't do it, we let His strength work through us and miracles happen.*

Recently I was agonizing over a situation that I was facing. I was worried that God might not come through and that the problems we were facing were just too big. I woke up in the middle of the night wondering if I'd promised too much. I had told everyone that God would provide, but now I wasn't so sure. My faith was failing, and it didn't feel good. As I lay there awake, I remembered how God had opened the doors for us to get to

Chapter 5: CONFIDENCE

Germany. He had worked out all the details in a way that I never could have imagined in advance.

I also remembered how our second son had been born three months premature. He faced a lot of physical challenges, including having heart surgery, but today he's fine. As we worried about his survival, we also faced hospital and doctor bills that totaled more than a quarter of a million dollars. The company I worked for had filed bankruptcy, and my insurance had been canceled shortly before our son was born.

One lawyer that I spoke with suggested that I keep my mouth shut, save $400, and file bankruptcy as soon as my son got out of the hospital. As I was sitting in the lawyer's office, God reminded me of the story of Jehoshaphat. When the armies came against him, Jehoshaphat was afraid and went to the Lord. I particularly like the last part of Jehoshaphat's prayer where he said, "For we have no power against this great multitude that is coming against us; nor do we know what to do, but our eyes are upon You" (2 Chron. 20:12).

Instead of taking this lawyer's advice, I trusted God. It took several months, but God worked out every detail. He led me to another lawyer who took our case and sued the company that had canceled my insurance. Before we ever got to trial, they settled out of court. All the bills got paid without us having to pay a penny.

God wants to display His power to the world and glorify His Name. He does it by putting us in situations — as He did with Jehoshaphat and a young kid named David —

where we are facing a giant and we don't have the strength or the knowledge to handle it ourselves. He does greater things than we could have imagined, because when we recognize that we can't do it, we let His strength work through us and miracles happen.

The Lion and the Bear

For most of his life David probably had no idea where God was leading him. The thought of becoming king may not have entered his mind until the day when God spoke to him and told him that he would become the commander of His people. God knew where He was leading David, even if David didn't have a clue. God had carefully orchestrated the events of David's life to prepare him for the steps that would lead him to become one of the greatest kings Israel would ever have.

God brings struggles, even battles, into our lives because He wants to strengthen our confidence and faith in Him. During trials and difficulties we get a chance to see whether our faith is strong or weak. We may not like it when our faith fails and our doubts and fears are exposed, but God remains faithful to us, helping us exercise and build our faith.

Throughout our lives we've heard things that have become ingrained in our thinking and firmly planted in our hearts. Most of what we heard was someone's opinions or experiences and not necessarily God's truth. We get to the point where we trust what we can see and understand rather than having faith in an invisible, all-powerful God. The result is that our hearts are full of unbelief. As our unbelief

Chapter 5: CONFIDENCE

becomes apparent, we have the opportunity to confront it with the truth. By doing that, we gradually replace the unbelief, doubts, and fears with hope and faith.

As David was growing up, I'm sure he heard all the stories about God delivering His people from Egypt. While watching his father's sheep, he probably spent hours thinking about God's power, maybe even turning some of his thoughts into poems and psalms of praise. He may even have imagined what it must have been like to stand at the edge of the Red Sea and to watch as God parted it, led Israel through to safety, and then closed the sea destroying Pharaoh's army. It must have been easy for him, like it is for most children, to believe that he, like Moses, could do great and mighty things for God.

When you ask kids what they want to become, most of them are more than happy to tell you that they want to be something great and exciting, like astronauts or superheroes. Nothing seems impossible until some well-meaning adults tell them that it's time to grow up, forget those crazy dreams, and face reality. We have to get older; it's just too bad that for most of us that also means losing our belief in the supernatural. Because people tell us that miracles don't happen, we stop believing in them.

In Matthew 18:3 Jesus tells us that we need to become like little children if we want to enter the kingdom of heaven. Part of the reason might be that we have to

Through these fights, God had prepared David's faith for a day when he would face a giant.

start believing in miracles again. Perhaps we need to stop thinking like rational adults who want to feel that everything is under control and we have it all figured out. If we can figure it out and handle it without God, then it won't be all that great and it definitely won't be miraculous. Like little children we need to start thinking about miracles and possibilities; we need to dream big dreams.

Somehow I doubt that it was normal for shepherds to grab lions and bears by their beards and kill them. Perhaps putting his life on the line for a couple of noisy, stupid sheep wasn't even a wise thing to do. Nonetheless, something in David compelled him to take action when the sheep were attacked. Unlike a paid servant, who probably would have run away, David not only stood his ground, but he also chased after the lion and the bear, saved his father's sheep, and defeated the predators with his bare hands.

David learned that God could give him victory over enemies that were stronger than he was. He learned that, with God, all things are possible. These battles confirmed what David had come to believe as a child: God is mighty and powerful and He was all the help David would ever need. Through these fights, God had prepared David's faith for a day when he would face a giant.

God knows where He wants to lead us. In His faithfulness, He brings situations into our lives that go beyond what we can handle on our own. He asks us to trust Him so that He can convince us that He will never fail us. Nothing strengthens our faith as much as having it tested in ever greater battles. When we read about the miracles that God performed in the Bible — maybe even vividly imagining Jesus healing the sick, giving sight to the blind and raising the dead — we create fertile soil in our hearts where our faith will grow. Not reading the Bible at all or rushing through our Bible reading, not letting the reality of God's power sink into our hearts, will leave our faith weak and full of doubt.

We face giants of different sizes throughout our lives. The giants we are facing today, no matter what form they take, are just one more battle in a series that God has been leading us to and through. It may feel like a giant leap compared to what we've experienced in the past; we may even think God is asking too much. The truth is that He always asks us to do more than we can handle on our own because He wants us to acknowledge our weakness and trust His strength.

Psalm 56:3 says: "Whenever I am afraid, I will trust in You." David was about to face the greatest battle of his life up to that point, with bigger battles and problems yet to come. The problems and battles were going to come whether he wanted them to or not. But David had learned how to make a conscious decision to have faith.

He knew that it wasn't about how he felt, because faith isn't a feeling — it's a decision. It's a choice we make that may go against our natural inclination. We learn how to choose faith in spite of our fears through what the Bible tells us and by remembering God's faithfulness as we experience His power every day.

Faith and Patience

Though David had already been anointed as king, he never forced his way to the throne. Even when he had the opportunity to kill Saul and become king, he refused to lift his hand against Saul, God's anointed. His friends encouraged him to take the chance, but he refused to do anything that would compromise his beliefs.

It's fear that makes us feel that we have to hurry, that we need to take matters into our own hands, or that the ends justify the means. David had enough faith in God to know that God would work things out. There was no reason for him to take shortcuts, especially shortcuts that would undermine his integrity.

Hebrews 6:12 tells us to imitate those who through faith and patience inherit the promises. In a tape I listened to, Rick Joyner commented that he was grateful for the faith movement and all that it had done to help the church, but he was still waiting for the patience movement.

The first few verses in James tell us that it is the testing of our faith that produces patience and that we need to let patience complete its work, so that we will be perfect and complete, lacking nothing. (James 1:2-4) Faith is the most powerful force in the universe, even to the point of allowing us to move mountains. But having faith doesn't mean we will get everything instantly.

If a farmer planted his seeds one day and tried to harvest them the next, we would think he was crazy. Farmers learn to be patient while they wait through the hot

Chapter 5: CONFIDENCE

summer months, fighting against drought, disease, and insects, until they can finally harvest their crops in the fall. God wants us to have a farmer's kind of faith — the kind of faith that withstands the trials and resists the doubts that threaten to ruin it.

> *Faith is powerful and patient at the same time. Faith moves mountains and it waits for harvests.*

Faith is a touchy subject for many because it's easy to feel condemned when we think or we're told that our faith is too small or not good enough. The Bible tells us that "faith is the substance of things hoped for" (Heb. 11:1) and that hope is something we don't yet see (Rom. 8:24). In other words, having faith doesn't mean we will have what we want in our hands. Faith is the patient expectation that causes what we hope for to be brought to us. It's our fear, our anxious thoughts, and not our faith that makes us feel we need immediate answers. Too often we miss the truth that faith and patience are two sides of the same coin.

Meditating on God's love is a powerful way to keep our faith strong, particularly when we have to wait on God. I sometimes question whether or not God still loves me when I don't get the answers to my prayers when and how I expect them. Then I realize that it is because He loves me that He asks me to add patience to my faith. He wants my faith to withstand every trial that I will face. He wants me to continue asking, keep seeking, and be constantly knocking. The answer may be that He will help me with His grace, rather than remove the problem, and that's OK. Having faith doesn't mean getting the answers I want when I want them. It means being patient, not giving up or taking matters into my own hands, until He answers.

On a practical note, I knew a pastor who used to say, "When you're sick, come for prayer and healing, but if you don't get healed, get help." That is still very good advice.

It's like the story about the man who gets caught in a flood. He prays and asks God to help him escape the flood and get to safety. Shortly after that a guy in a rowboat comes by and asks if he needs help. He replies that he's fine and that God will help him, so the guy in the boat rows away. The water continues to rise and the man finds himself up on his roof, clinging to his chimney, crying out to God for help. A helicopter comes along, and the pilot yells down to the man offering help. He replies that he's OK, God will help him.

The water continues to rise, and the man ends up drowning. As he stands before God, he's very upset and demands to know why God didn't help him. God replies, "But I sent you a rowboat and a helicopter. What were you expecting Me to do?"

Having faith and patience didn't mean that David sat around and did nothing. During the time between his fight with Goliath and the time when he was finally recognized as king, he continued to fight God's enemies and help God's people. He was a king, doing what kings should do, long before he ever sat on a throne or wore a crown.

It seems we often get it backwards. We think that once we have a crown and we're sitting on a throne, then we'll be kings and we'll finally do what kings do. But David realized it was about God's anointing, doing what God wanted him to do, and not about getting recognition from other people. In faith, he began acting like a king the minute he received the anointing. He knew that he would become the official king in God's perfect timing.

Hebrews 11:1 says, "Now faith is the substance of things hoped for, the evidence of things not seen." Our hope may not be visible in the physical or outer world, but we do see it in our minds. We hold fast to the image of what we hope for, knowing that God will bring it to pass in His time.

My simple formula for faith is: desire + expectation + action = faith. The desire (our hope) is mixed with the expectation (the substance) in our minds that we will have what we seek. The evidence is seen in what we do and say, because we begin to think and act in a way that expresses our faith right now. In other words, when we have faith, we immediately begin to adopt the attitudes and actions that are consistent with our hope. We live today as if we already have what is still unseen.

Jack Nicklaus, one of the greatest golfers who ever lived, once said that he never hit a shot until after he had seen it in his mind. I enjoy playing golf and I find that my best shots are the ones that I clearly see in my mind before I take my swing.

Having a clear picture in our minds that we constantly repeat, like the map of Germany we had on our dining room wall so many years ago, helps us see ourselves already there. By seeing ourselves possessing what we hope for, we unconsciously act as if we already have what we want, and we hasten its realization.

David's faith not only enabled him to win battles against gigantic odds, but it also enabled him to behave like a king while he waited patiently for God to fulfill the promise He had made to him. Faith is powerful and patient at the same time. Faith moves mountains and it waits for harvests. It is built on His word, strengthened through our struggles, convinced of His love, and sure of His promises.

Taking Action

There are times when our faith seems to falter because we are actually expecting something completely different from what we are hoping and praying to receive. We might pray for healing but still expect to be sick the next morning so that we won't have to go to work. James 1:5-8 tells us that someone who doubts, whose thoughts are divided between two different desires, will not receive anything from God. It even goes on to say that a double-minded person is unstable in everything. I'll talk more about commitment later, but we do have to cover one point now. The most important thing we can do for our faith is to make a firm decision for something. As long as we are going back and forth in our minds, our faith will be full of doubt.

We should always expect God to answer our prayers through other people in ways that will bring blessing and increase to both them and us.

It's actually better to be firmly committed to something than to be torn between multiple options. David didn't allow his thoughts to waver when he faced Goliath. He knew that God could help him defeat Goliath, and he refused to entertain any other thoughts. Whatever you are seeking from God, decide now that you will hold firmly to the desire, create a clear picture in your mind in which you see yourself having and enjoying it, and then begin to give thanks for it now.

Memorize and meditate on scriptures like Mark 11:22-24 or Luke 11:9-10. I find it interesting that Jesus used the word *assuredly* in Mark 11:23. That word is translated as *verily* in the King James Version, and it means "truly." In other words, He is saying, "What I am about to tell you is truth." The truth is that we can have whatever we ask for when we believe and don't doubt.

James 4:1-3 offers one caveat. The people to whom James was writing had gotten to the point in their covetous lusts that they were willing to murder people in order to get what they wanted. It always bothers me when people use these verses in James to tell us that we can't have what we want. James isn't telling us that we can't have what we desire; he's showing us how to ask for it properly.

When we pray in faith to receive something from God, it's never about taking it away from someone else. In other words, we are not to covet what others have. We look to God, the Creator, to supply our needs from His riches in glory, not from our neighbor's bank account. We just need to remember that it's OK to ask God to help us create the income so that we can have cars similar to our neighbors', but we can't ask God to take our neighbors' cars away from them and give them to us.

Also, we can't expect God to simply drop things in our lap. God will normally bring the things we expect to us through the already established methods of supply. As I pointed out in the story about the man in the flood, our prayers will be answered through people that we know or meet. We should always expect God to answer our prayers through other people in ways that will bring blessing and increase to both them and us.

CHAPTER 6

Creativity – Using Our Imagination

Chapter 6

Creativity — Using Our Imagination

So Saul clothed David with his armor, and he put a bronze helmet on his head; he also clothed him with a coat of mail. David fastened his sword to his armor and tried to walk, for he had not tested them. And David said to Saul, "I cannot walk with these, for I have not tested them." So David took them off.

Then he took his staff in his hand; and he chose for himself five smooth stones from the brook, and put them in a shepherd's bag, in a pouch which he had, and his sling was in his hand. And he drew near to the Philistine.
~ 1 Samuel 17:38-40

The trend in the consumer market has been that luxuries become commodities. In other words, the products that only a few could afford eventually become necessities that everyone must have. What was once available only to the rich becomes commonplace.

> Henry Ford didn't invent the automobile. What he discovered was a way to mass-produce them.

The computer is a great example. At one point computers were physically huge, and only a handful of universities and large companies had them. Ken Olsen, the founder of Digital Equipment Corporation, made the company famous by inventing the departmental computer. This allowed every department in a company to have their own, rather than having to fight for time on the company's mainframe. But Ken was also famous for saying, "There is no reason for any individual to have a computer in his home." It just goes to show that even some of the best innovators need to change with the times and continue to innovate.

The movement of goods from luxuries to commodities and from expensive to affordable is good for consumers. As prices get lower, the standard of living goes up. It can be hard on businesses, though, since it often means that the margins go down while competition increases. Innovation becomes essential to survival. Companies that settle for selling commodities end up in price wars that force them to find increasingly more efficient ways to manufacture and market their products.

In the first chapter of Genesis, we read that God created mankind in His own image and placed them in the Garden of Eden. In Genesis 1:28 God commanded them, "Be fruitful and multiply; fill the earth and subdue it; have dominion over the fish of the sea, over the birds of the air, and over every living thing that moves on the earth." "Be fruitful and multiply" has to do with procreation, but it also has much broader implications.

God put man in the garden so that he could tend it. Another connotation of being fruitful is to work in the garden so that it bears more fruit and is more productive. When God said to "multiply" in that context, it means that

He wants us not only to add to our production, but also to multiply our productivity.

When we apply this commandment to every area of our lives, and in particular to our careers and businesses, it raises some interesting questions. For example, we could ask the question: How can we produce twice as much in the same amount of time? Even better, we might ask: How can we be more productive in less time and at a lower cost? The fastest way for a business to multiply its profit is to serve more people in less time and with lower expenses. The best way for an employee to succeed on the job is to continually improve his productivity.

Henry Ford didn't invent the automobile; he discovered a way to mass-produce them. He figured out how to make hundreds of cars in a day, rather than just one. Because he allowed each worker to do only one thing, he no longer needed highly skilled craftsmen working on all the facets of a single car. All he needed was for someone to learn one task and do it over and over on a hundred cars. He learned how to produce more in the same amount of time with lower costs. The result was that the automobile went from a luxury that only a few could afford to a commodity that everyone wanted; to a necessity we feel we can't live without today.

I've heard people say that we all get three or four ideas a year that could be worth millions or that would dramatically improve our lives. We might get ideas for a new business or ways we can improve our existing jobs. We might think of things we can do that will benefit our families and improve our personal lives. Most of the ideas hit us while we're in the shower, and we forget them by the time our hair is dry.

Unfortunately, we often discount our ideas. We assume that no one will listen to us or that the idea wasn't that great. We think about the potential pain of rejection or embarrassment if we share our ideas with anyone, and that's the end of them. Most of us remember a time when we were young and the other kids laughed at our novel ideas, so we vowed that we would never make that mistake again.

> *God gave us the ability to be creative. We can imagine things that don't exist and figure out ways to build them.*

We forget that we were created in God's image. God gave us the ability to be creative. We can imagine things that don't exist and figure out ways to build them. Jim Rohn talks about turning nothing into something — in other words, taking an intangible idea and turning it into a product. In our minds we create the image of a house, then using some raw materials, along with our labor and skill, we build it.

As children we were all creative geniuses. We could have the most amazing adventures in our backyards with just a few pieces of wood simply by using our imaginations. Perhaps another benefit of becoming like little children, as Jesus told us in Matthew 18:3, is that we reconnect not just with our inner child, but also with our inner creator. We revive our imaginations.

In his audio program *Lead the Field*, Earl Nightingale talks about spending twenty minutes a day just thinking. He suggests finding a quiet place, maybe taking a cup of coffee, and sitting down with a legal pad and a pen. At the top of a clean page we should write down a problem to solve or a goal to reach, then fill in the rest of the page, writing down as many ideas as we can think of that relate to the problem or goal.

It can also help if we take some time before going to bed each night to think and pray, asking God to give us the wisdom to solve the problems we're facing or reach the goals we're pursuing. Doing it right before bed also gives our subconscious minds time to work on the problem or goal while we sleep. Many people find that they wake up the next morning with an idea that can help solve the problem.

An experiment was done at a school with two pottery classes. The first class was told that their objective for the term was to create just one perfect pot. The other class was told that they were to make as many pots as possible during that term. None of the kids in the first class were able to make a perfect pot, but the kids in the other class were able to create lots of them.

When it comes to our ideas, quantity is the most important thing. Our attitude needs to be: Any and every idea is good, at least initially. Some of them will end up being impractical in the long run, and others just plain won't work. But even the worst idea can act as a catalyst that may lead to some good ideas.

One of the advantages of brainstorming is that a lot of ideas are generated when several people are working on the same problem. Just remember the one cardinal rule of a good brainstorming session: No one is allowed to suggest that the problem can't be solved. Anyone who starts talking about what won't work needs to be reminded that such suggestions don't help, and the group needs to immediately get back to generating lots of constructive ideas.

Let me add one caution: Some people suffer from idea avalanche. They get so many ideas that they never finish anything. Partway through something, another great idea comes along, and off they go. Instead of running off with every new idea or forgetting them all together, we can write them down in notebooks or journals where we can keep track of them.

All around my house I have legal pads as well as journals that I use to write down any ideas that come to me. I even have one in my nightstand along with a pencil and a small flashlight. When I get an idea in the middle of the night, I can write it down immediately. Never fool yourself into believing that you'll remember it in the morning; always write it down. As someone once said, "The dullest pencil is better than the sharpest mind."

One of the important elements of success is focus. Some things take a while before they begin to bear fruit. We have to be careful not to abandon them too soon simply because some new idea caught our attention. We should stick with one thing until it's running well. Many people fail because they jump from one thing to another and never do anything long enough to become successful at it.

Saul's Armor

Proverbs 15:22 tells us, "Without counsel, plans go awry, but in the multitude of counselors they are established." Proverbs 20:18 (KJV) says, "Every purpose is established by counsel; and with good advice make war." There's wisdom in talking with people and getting counsel from them — asking them for advice so that we avoid costly mistakes and improve our chances for success. The more information we can gather before we do something, the better. Occasionally, however, we run into a problem when people not only want to offer their advice, but they also want to tell us exactly how we need to do things.

First Samuel 9:2 tells us that Saul was literally head and shoulders above all the people. Since he was so tall, I find it interesting that in 1 Samuel 17:38-39, he offered his armor to David. It should have been clear to him that it would be much too big and that David would be swimming in it. If anything, wearing Saul's armor was likely to cause problems for David.

Maybe Saul was just trying to help. He realized that David didn't have his own armor, and because Saul wasn't going to be using his, it may have just been a nice gesture to let David borrow it. I don't really know. But there will be times when people will offer some well-meaning

> *The world's economy runs on the philosophy that says there is only so much to go around and that if I'm going to get what I want, someone else will have to do without. In God's economy, the only shortage is a shortage of ideas.*

advice or "help" that doesn't fit or work for us. When that happens, we just need to do what David did and not let it get in our way.

Earlier I said that Saul's warning to David 1 Samuel 17:33 was good advice. He reminded David that he was a youth, but Goliath had been "a man of war from his youth." In the business world we might say that if David were going to win, he would have to minimize his weaknesses (the fact that he wasn't a warrior) and maximize his strengths. David was not going to be able to fight Goliath using the traditional methods; he was going to have to innovate.

From the reactions of all the other soldiers when they saw Goliath, I'm sure they assumed that the battle would be fought with sword, shield, and spear. No wonder they were afraid. It was obvious to all of them that a normal person in a one-on-one battle would never be able to get close to Goliath, let alone kill him. In that sense, it was good that David wasn't a warrior. It forced him to look for some other way to fight Goliath.

I wonder if he took a quick inventory of his skills to see if he could come up with some ideas. He could play the harp really well, so he might have been able to calm Goliath's nerves, like he did when Saul was troubled by an evil spirit (1 Sam. 16:14-23). However, that wouldn't help David defeat him. He was also a pretty good shepherd, but he didn't want to lead Goliath to greener pastures; he wanted to bury him under one. So, what was left?

Fortunately, David had learned how to use a sling. He had enough confidence in his skill with it that he felt sure he could defeat Goliath. Using a sling in battle wasn't new. Judges 20:16 tells us that there were hundreds of men who were deadly accurate with a sling. Again, it seems everyone must have been assuming they would have to fight Goliath with a sword, because no one else came up with the idea of using a sling except a young shepherd boy who had to think a little "outside the box" if he was going to have any chance of survival.

Romans 12:2 tells us that we should not conform to the world — what everybody else thinks and does — but instead we should be transformed by the renewing of our minds. The Bible teaches us many things that are contrary to the way most people think life is supposed to work.

The world's economy runs on the philosophy that says there is only so much to go around and that if I'm going to get what I want, someone else will have to do without. In God's economy, the only shortage is a shortage of ideas. God made sure that there was more than enough for everybody to have their fair share. As we use our imaginations, we will find new ways to create more for the benefit of everyone.

While most people believe in scarcity, we are told that Christ came to give us life and abundance (John 10:10). When we live in abundance we view the world in a very different way. While everyone else thinks that they have to fight for their piece of the pie, the Bible teaches us that we receive from God's riches in glory, from His abundance.

James 4:1 asks, "Where do wars and fights come from among you?" James answers his own question by writing that they come from the desire for pleasures and the lusts that war within us. As I mentioned earlier, he goes on to say that people were resorting to murder so that they could take the things they wanted. They didn't realize that the only thing they needed to do was to ask.

We aren't limited to traditional ways of thinking. We don't have to keep doing things a certain way because "that's how it's always been done." God created us in His image and gave us the ability to think. He also gave us the responsibility to use our imaginations and to come up with new ways to solve our problems that will result in blessing and abundance for everyone.

Nothing New Under the Sun

When I first starting reading the Bible, I was very confused by the verses in Ecclesiastes 1:9-10 which say, "That which has been is what will be, that which is done is what will be done, And there is nothing new under the sun. Is there anything of which it may be said, 'See, this is new'? It has already been in ancient times before us."

> *The only thing that prevented Solomon from having a 747 was his lack of awareness of how to use the materials and laws that were available to him.*

I thought that this statement must be wrong because we have airplanes, and Solomon, who wrote Ecclesiastes, didn't have them. But then someone pointed out that we don't have anything that couldn't have been invented much earlier. The natural laws that govern how a plane flies have always been there. Even the materials that are used are made from raw materials that have been there all along. And the man-made materials could have been created sooner as well.

The only thing that prevented Solomon from having a 747 was his lack of awareness of how to use the materials and laws that were available to him. People weren't aware of this because they hadn't yet felt the need. After all, when your world is small and flat, a horse is fast enough to get you from one end to the other.

In chapter 2, I talked about a prayer that I had prayed when faced with a difficult problem at work. In that prayer I said, "Lord, man invented computers, and you created man. Surely You can help me figure out what's wrong here." We need to recognize that God knows all that there is to know; He already has the answer to every question or problem we might face.

Proverbs 25:2 says, "It is the glory of God to conceal a matter, but the glory of kings is to search out a matter." The answers we are looking for can be found, but we have to want to find them. All the knowledge, understanding, and wisdom we need are waiting for us. The first chapter of Proverbs even tells us that wisdom is crying out to us, offering to put a spirit of wisdom upon us, but that we often refuse to listen.

When I was young I heard that "curiosity killed the cat." I wondered why anyone would say something like that. Maybe it was just a frustrated adult who had become tired of answering all my questions! But if we take that proverb to heart, we might think that being curious could be detrimental to our health. Maybe we should stop asking questions and just accept the facts as they're handed to us. After all, two plus two equals four, and that's all we need to know, right? I don't think so!

I wonder how different the story of David and Goliath would have been if David had put on Saul's armor and faced Goliath with a sword and spear. I doubt that we'd be talking about it now, because it would have just been a short story about a little kid with a big mouth who was killed by a giant. Instead of learning how the little guy beat the odds, we'd be reminded that we shouldn't bite off more than we can chew.

David knew that God would provide not only the strength but also the wisdom he needed to defeat Goliath. Because God knows everything, we never have to worry about not knowing what to do when we face our problems. All the answers we will ever need are available to us right now; all we have to do is be willing to look for them.

In Proverbs, Solomon tells us that wisdom is more precious than rubies or anything else that we might desire (Prov. 3:15). The smartest thing we can do is to look to God and seek His wisdom as if it were a hidden treasure (Prov. 2:4). Second Chronicles 1:15 says that Solomon "made silver and gold as common in Jerusalem as stones." Perhaps part of the reason we will have everything we need when we seek God's kingdom first (Matt. 6:33) is that we will find all the wisdom necessary so that we can live abundantly in every area of our lives, even financially.

Five Smooth Stones

I don't know if there was a specific reason or if there is some significant symbolism that explains why David took five stones. The logical reason is pretty clear, though. David would have been foolish, even arrogant, to go in to battle with only one stone.

I'm sure he was hoping that he would only have to use one stone, but he was smart enough to not make assumptions. There was a good chance that if the first stone simply bounced off, Goliath would have been really mad. If that had happened, David would have been under a lot of pressure to reload his sling quickly or be killed.

It would be great if being really creative meant that we'd hit a home run the first time and every time we tried something. Like David, we need to be smart enough to know that the odds are against it. A home run is wonderful when it happens, but we shouldn't count on it. Like the pottery class that made a lot of pots, the best way to make sure that we succeed is to keep trying. Quantity will win out every time, because each mistake or setback will give us valuable feedback for the next time. As long as we keep trying, we will get better.

How many times are we going to fail before we become successful? When we watch little children learn how to walk, we naturally assume that they'll stumble and fall. As long as the child is reasonably healthy, we would never say, "Well, I guess that kid will never learn how to walk." It sounds pretty silly when we're talking about a child learning how to walk, but for some reason when it comes to our own success, many of us would rather just crawl around on the floor the rest of our lives than to risking falling even once. Maybe the question should be: Why would I ever stop trying? As Les Brown says, "It ain't over until you win."[1]

> *It sounds pretty silly when we're talking about a child learning how to walk but for some reason, when it comes to our own success, many of us would rather just crawl around on the floor the rest of our lives than to fall even once.*

Not only did David have five stones; those stones were smooth. The stones had been in the stream long enough that all the rough edges had been worn off. Years ago I worked for someone who had a quote from Einstein on her office wall: "If you can't explain it simply, you don't understand it well enough."

It's important to work with our ideas long enough that they become simple. The more complicated something is, the more likely it is that things will go wrong. The most ingenious solutions are usually the simplest.

As my wife keeps pointing out to me, there comes a time when we have to stop polishing the stones and put them in the sling. I believe that it was General George Patton who once said, "I'd rather have a good plan violently executed today than have the perfect plan tomorrow." The time will come — and for most of us it will be sooner than we think — when we've learned all the theory we can. At that time, all the additional knowledge and understanding will come by learning from the mistakes and successes we experience. There are many questions that we don't even know about until we try to do something. The sooner we get started, the sooner we'll be able to gain the wisdom we need in order to learn and become successful.

God has given us an abundant world, full of opportunity. Because He's given us the ability to create, there's no need for us to compete. We can use our imaginations combined with labor and turn our ideas into realities. We can use our unique gifts and abilities, then seek advice and counsel that we adapt to our strengths so that our plans will succeed.

We will always face new problems, but the source for the solutions to those problems will always be the same. All the wisdom we will ever need is available to us through God. When we seek Him first, everything we need will be given to us (Matt. 6:33).

Taking Action

There are two concepts that may seem to be in conflict, but they really work well together: stick with one thing until we really understand it, and get varied input.

The first concept is to stick with one thing and study it thoroughly until we really understand it. One of the reasons I like to meditate on a particular Scripture for months at a time, maybe even years, is because I always gain new understanding when I do that. I see new things because of how I've changed and grown, and that Scripture becomes a part of me.

Some years ago I took a class at work called "Becoming an Everyday Genius." The class taught me some valuable tools, like mind mapping, which was created by Tony Buzan. For more information on mind mapping go to: www.mind-map.com.

One of the most interesting things I learned in the class was about how we remember, or more correctly how easily we forget, the information we learn from a seminar or book. It's normal to forget up to 90 percent of what we've learned within a few days, but by reviewing the information at regular intervals, it's actually possible to learn more than 100 percent of what was taught. When we start to incorporate the information into our way of thinking and combine it with information from other sources, we learn more than what we originally heard.

When we want to really understand something, it's best to review the information we have on a regular basis over a long period of time. That way we'll gain additional insights from other things that we hear and learn later, as well as make new connections with information we already have.

The other concept is to get varied input. That can come by seeking advice or simply by changing our environment. For example, going outside, getting some fresh air, and marveling at God's creation may give us fresh insights into the problems we're dealing with. If you're stuck on a problem, listen to some classical music and contemplate a tree. In other words, get your mind out of the rut and open yourself up to new possibilities.

Napoleon Hill, the author of *Think and Grow Rich* was given the opportunity to interview five hundred of the world's most successful people. One of the people he interviewed was Thomas Edison. In an audio program Hill talked about Edison trying over and over to find a way to make the light bulb work. I've heard estimates that he tried over ten thousand different things. According to Hill, the breakthrough came when Edison thought about how charcoal is made by burning wood in the absence of oxygen. When Edison removed the oxygen, the modern lightbulb was born.

Sometimes that great idea we're searching for will come to us when we've done all the studying we can, tried as hard as we can to fully understand something, and then started doing things that are totally unrelated. When we let our conscious minds do something else, God can speak to us through our subconscious minds and give us the answer. Concentrating on something and learning all we can is still necessary, but the breakthrough may come to us "out of the blue," usually when we're relaxed and not worrying about the problem.

> *Concentrating on something and learning all we can is still necessary, but the breakthrough may come to us "out of the blue," usually when we're relaxed and not worrying about the problem.*

I brought this up earlier, but it bears repeating. It's important that we keep a journal of our thoughts and ideas. Michael Gelb, author of *How to Think Like Leonardo da Vinci*, said in an interview that people that he has studied — people we recognize as geniuses — were all in the habit of keeping a journal. While we might think that they kept a journal because they were geniuses, the truth may be that they were geniuses because they kept a journal.

I realized some time ago that in order to have more of something in life, it's important to put a high value on it. In other words, if I want more ideas, then I need to value and respect the ones I currently have. If I don't have enough respect for my ideas to take the time to write them down, then I will end up having fewer of them. Furthermore, if I don't respect them, it's unlikely that anyone else will respect them.

Most of our ideas and thoughts come as answers to the questions we ask ourselves. This is why it's a bad idea to ask the question: "Why do I keep failing?" The answer to that question may be easy to find, but do we really want our minds dwelling on why we keep failing? It might be better to ask the question in a more positive way: "What can I do right now that will help me become more successful?" The answer to that question may take a little longer to find, but it will be much more helpful.

Our ideas come from answers that God gives us to the questions we ask. If we want to improve our lives, we just need to start asking better questions, or at least different questions. Then we need to have respect for the answers and ideas that we get by writing them down. It's possible that the breakthrough we've been looking for — the wisdom for how we can slay our Goliath — is just one idea away.

CHAPTER 7

Commitment – Making Decisions

Chapter 7

Commitment — Making Decisions

So it was, when the Philistine arose and came and drew near to meet David, that David hurried and ran toward the army to meet the Philistine. Then David put his hand in his bag and took out a stone; and he slung it and struck the Philistine in his forehead, so that the stone sank into his forehead, and he fell on his face to the earth. So David prevailed over the Philistine with a sling and a stone, and struck the Philistine and killed him. But there was no sword in the hand of David. Therefore David ran and stood over the Philistine, took his sword and drew it out of its sheath and killed him, and cut off his head with it.

And when the Philistines saw that their champion was dead, they fled. ~ 1 Samuel 17:48-51

In Matthew 25:14-30, we read about the parable of the talents. Before going on a long journey, a man called three of his servants and gave each of them a different number of talents. He gave five talents to one servant, two to another, and just one to the third servant, based on their individual abilities. A talent in gold would be worth more than a million dollars today, so even the servant with only one talent received a substantial sum of money. When the man returned from his journey, he called his three servants and asked them to tell him what they had done with the talents they had been given.

The first two servants told the master they had used the talents and had doubled them. It appears that they had used their imaginations and labors and had multiplied what they originally received. Then the third servant came in and started making excuses. He explained that he understood that his master was a hard man. He knew that the master expected to get back more than he had given, but because the servant was afraid that he might lose the master's talent, he had hidden it.

The master became very angry and said, "You wicked and lazy servant, you knew that I reap where I have not sown, and gather where I have not scattered seed. So you ought to have deposited my money with the bankers, and at my coming I would have received back my own with interest" (Matt. 25:26-27). He then took the talent from him, and gave it to the one who had turned five talents into ten.

> *The servant had received only what the master knew he could handle. Apparently the servant had a lot less faith in his abilities than his master had.*

If we broaden the meaning of talents to the English word *talents*, that is, gifts or natural abilities, rather than a sum of money, it's possible to apply this parable to most of our lives. A time will come when we, as the servants, will stand before our master, Jesus, and tell Him what we did with our lives. It's possible that He'll ask us what we did with our money, but it's also likely that He will ask us, "What did you do with the gifts and abilities I gave you?"

Chapter 7: COMMITMENT

The servant who hid his talent said that he was afraid of losing it. However, he had received the talent based on his abilities. The master wasn't setting him up for failure. The servant had received only what the master knew he could handle. Apparently the servant had a lot less faith in his abilities than his master had.

The sad part is that he did lose the talent — not because he tried something and failed, but because he allowed his fear to control his decisions. Rather than deciding in faith to use what his master had given him, he made a bad decision out of fear.

There are times in sporting events when a team will become defensive. I don't mean that a team has its defensive personnel on the field; what I mean is that they begin playing to prevent a loss rather than playing to win the game. This usually ends up going like it did for the servant who hid his talent. The thing that they feared happens, and they end up losing the game to the team that played to win.

It's interesting that the Bible doesn't explain what would have happened if the servant had poorly invested his talent and lost it. I don't know if we can always draw a conclusion from what the Bible doesn't say, but in this case I have to wonder if it means that we can't lose unless we refuse to play the game. In other words, when we have faith and use what God has given us, our success is virtually guaranteed.

Most people will fail in life simply because they never decide to be successful. They may allow the fear of failure to actually cause them to fail because they don't make decisions that would help them succeed. They seem to forget that Jesus wants us to do something with our talents. He wants us to have faith and use them so that we can increase them, even multiply them, and give them all back to Him for His glory.

Maybe some people assume that things will work out by default — that God will do what He wants to do and all we have to do is sit back and watch. In other words they believe that we don't have to be actively involved because God is in control of our lives. Some may even be afraid of making decisions because they wouldn't want to do something that would mess up God's will for them.

I'm reminded of the Israelites who came out of Egypt. After they heard the report about the Promised Land — that the land devoured its inhabitants and that it was full of giants (Num. 13:32-33) — they chose to listen to their fears. Joshua and Caleb tried to convince the people that all they would have to do was enter the land and victory would be theirs. They simply had to decide to believe that God had given them the land and enter it, and success was guaranteed. That generation died in the wilderness because they refused to believe God. They acted out of fear, rather than faith, and they lost the blessings God wanted to give them.

Making decisions isn't easy; some people even fear making them. It's not about good or bad decisions as much as it is about making any decision. Jim Rohn says, "Indecision is the thief of opportunity."[1] James 1:8 tells us that the double-minded man is unstable in all his ways. He won't receive anything from God because he is like the waves of the sea, continually tossed by the wind. He's torn between different things and he can't decide which one he wants.

Chapter 7: COMMITMENT

Making a clear decision can scare us because it limits our options. It's like looking at the menu and seeing five or six meals that we like, but knowing that we have to pick just one of them. The Germans have an expression, "Qual der Wahl" (pronounced: kvahl dare vahl), which means the pain of choice. The more choices we have — especially when all of them appeal to us — the harder it is to choose one of them.

Yogi Berra says, "When you come to a fork in the road, take it." This is how a lot of people appear to approach their decisions. By desperately trying to keep their options open, they end up deciding not to decide, and they lose all the benefits of all the possible choices. An interviewer once asked Bill Cosby about the key to success. He said, "I don't know the key to success, but the key to failure is to try to please everyone."

To be successful, we have to make decisions. It may not be easy or popular, but we still have to make them. Even a bad decision is better than no decision.

There's a story about a young CEO who wanted to be sure that he did the best job he could, so he met with an old CEO and asked him if he had any advice. The old CEO looked at him and said, "I have two words for you: good decisions." The young CEO thought about it for a minute, and asked, "But how do I make good decisions?" The old CEO replied, "I have one word for you: experience." Again the young CEO thought for a moment and then asked, "But how do I get experience?" The old CEO smiled and said, "I have two words for you: bad decisions."

Bernie Fuchs said, "Commitment is a line you must cross . . . it is the difference between dreaming and doing." Dreams that we don't act on are just daydreams. They may be entertaining, but they don't have much value for us. We have to look at our dreams and decide to act on them. If we don't take action, we become like the lazy man in Proverbs 21:25 whose desires kill him, because his hands refuse to labor.

The Acorn and the Oak Tree

> *The acorn's real strength — the thing that guarantees its success — is the fact that it knows exactly what it wants to be when it grows up; it never changes its mind.*

Bob Proctor, who wrote *You Were Born Rich*, has spent the last forty years teaching people how to discover the greatness that is in them. In an interview he discussed the common saying that "the oak tree is in the acorn." Bob pointed out that there is no oak tree in the acorn, and all you have to do is to cut one open and look inside. If you do, you won't find an oak tree. The oak tree is actually in the universe. If it's planted in the ground, the acorn will attract all the nutrients, or energy, that it needs to grow and become an oak tree.

If the acorn were like most people, I doubt that it would ever grow into anything. Can you imagine the acorn saying to itself, "I don't want to be an oak tree; I think I'd rather be an orange tree. No, wait a minute, the climate here isn't conducive to growing an orange tree; maybe I should become an apple tree instead. No, that won't work either, because I don't really want to lose my leaves in the fall, so I think I'll become a pine tree." A conversation like that would be pretty ridiculous for an acorn.

Not being acorns gives humans some advantages, but it also creates some problems. The acorn's real strength — the thing that guarantees its success — is the fact that it knows exactly what it wants to be when it grows up; it never changes its mind. While the oak tree isn't in the acorn, the pattern or plan for one is. God has placed in the acorn all the information, as well as the energy needed to attract everything necessary for its growth.

If we take another look at the parable of the talents from Matthew 25, we'll see that God has given us, his servants, all that we need in order to be successful. The gifts and abilities, along with the energy we need to attract everything else necessary for our growth, are in us already. The only thing that is lacking is a clear decision on our part — a commitment to use what God has placed within us. We are not to bury our gifts in the ground like the servant who received just one talent. Instead we need to use our gifts in the marketplace like the two servants who multiplied their talents.

When we couple our commitment and our faith, God will begin to bring to us everything we need for our success. In Mark 11:22-24, Jesus tells us that we can have anything we want if we will just believe and not doubt. We doubt when we are torn between different desires and when we refuse to make or commit to a decision.

A Sense of Urgency

When the phone rang, I looked at the clock next to the bed. It was shortly after 4:00 A.M. and I hoped that this was a wrong number. My younger brother's wife, Valerie, was on the other end. She was crying and telling me how sorry she was. What she was saying didn't make any sense to me, because she seemed to be telling me that my brother Peter had died. I couldn't believe it. At age forty-six, my little brother, who had appeared to be the picture of good health, had died of a massive heart attack in the middle of the night.

I got up and called my other brothers, who were just as shocked by the news as I was. None of us could believe this had happened. My wife had gone to visit her sister, so I called her quickly, and gave her the news. Then I threw some clothes together and started the two-and-a-half hour drive to Peter's house.

On the way there I began to think about the defining moments in life — those times when circumstances or events seem to shake us to the core. From that point on, things are never the same.

One of our holiday traditions had been that we would drive to Peter's for Christmas, and he and his family would spend New Year's Eve at our house. For several years in a row we had found movies that Peter and his family really enjoyed. About two or three weeks before he died, I had been thinking about the upcoming New Year's Eve. It was only the beginning of April, but I wanted to be sure to keep my eyes open for a good movie that I was sure they'd really enjoy. I was already looking forward to this annual tradition.

Chapter 7: COMMITMENT

We have to be careful that we don't take time for granted. Something Jim Rohn talks about really hit home the week of Peter's funeral. It's a way of looking at how much time we have in life. For example, parents may need to realize that the kids are getting older. The time will come, and sooner than most parents of toddlers think, when the kids will no longer be joining Mom and Dad on vacation. Instead of saying, "We take a family vacation every year," they may want to say, "We'll take ten or twelve more family vacations before the kids will be too old."

We need to develop a sense of urgency. Psalm 90:12 says, "So teach us to number our days, that we may gain a heart of wisdom." We need the wisdom to use and invest our time, rather than to simply spend it, waste it, or kill it.

After David made his decision, he didn't waste any time. The smartest thing for him to do was to act immediately. He probably didn't want to spend too much time thinking about his decision. If he had spent more time thinking about it, he might have talked himself out of fighting Goliath. Instead, David didn't just step out in faith; he ran! It's like the saying about having to eat a frog: If you're going to have to eat a frog anyway, you might as well do it fast, because it's never going to look any better!

> *We need to develop a sense of urgency. Psalm 90:12 says, "So teach us to number our days, that we may gain a heart of wisdom." The wisdom to use and invest our time, rather than to simply spend it, waste it, or kill it.*

If I had been the one facing a giant, I might have been tempted to read one more book about being a warrior before I went out on the battlefield, or I'd have thought about going to the practice range with my sling and throwing a couple of buckets of stones, just to be sure I was using the proper technique. There's nothing I love more about work than putting it off, and I usually have a lot of good reasons. I can be like the lazy man in Proverbs 26:16, who thinks he's smarter than seven sensible people.

A farmer may want and need to harvest a good crop. But unless he's willing to work: to till the soil, plant the seed, and care for it, he won't have a harvest. There comes time when we have to act.

One of my favorite stories from the Old Testament is the story of Jacob in Genesis 32. Esau and Jacob were twin brothers. Esau had been born first, and all the rights of the firstborn were his, but Jacob had cheated him out of the birthright and the blessing that went along with it. Naturally, Esau was angry and wanted to kill Jacob, so Jacob ran away. Now, many years later, Jacob was returning home.

Jacob sent one of his servants to find Esau and to tell him that he was coming. The servant returned and said that he delivered the message to Esau, and that Esau was now on his way to meet Jacob with four hundred men.

Considering that Jacob had cheated Esau, it wasn't hard for Jacob to assume that the four hundred men weren't a welcoming committee. He was scared, so he started sending gifts to Esau. Jacob also divided his family into two groups, and sent them ahead on separate trails hoping that

Chapter 7: Commitment

if Esau came across one of them, he would only destroy half of his family. Jacob ended up spending the night wrestling with God in order to get a blessing from Him. He received the blessing he wanted, and God changed his name from Jacob, which means someone who uses treachery to take what he wants, to Israel, which means someone who has power or has prevailed with God.

Not only had his name changed, but he was also a changed man. In wrestling with God he had shown great faith and patience, even tenacity. His wrestling match was another struggle that God had led him to and through, and he was ready for what would happen when he faced Esau.

I have no idea how Jacob, now called Israel, felt as he stood there alone waiting for Esau and his army to arrive. I have to assume that he had faith that God's blessing would get him through the day and that he would not die. He put himself in a position that left him no means of escape. This time, he was not going to run away.

Sometimes running away can take a variety of forms. It might be something as simple as turning on the TV for a few mindless hours of channel surfing. I find that entertainment can be a great way to escape the pressure of working on my dreams. My mind is fully occupied and I might even find something educational. But if I'm going to make progress on my dreams, I have to be like Jacob. I have to be willing to put myself in a position where I have to take action, where I can't run away.

I'm not recommending that anyone quit his job. There are plenty of ways to put pressure on ourselves to act on our dreams that don't involve creating financial burdens. It may be as simple as making some realistic schedules, setting aside time when we're not at work, and making ourselves accountable to someone who will hold us to the schedule.

Having a sense of urgency means knowing that life is short and there's no time to waste. It also means that there will come a time — and it may be sooner than we might like — when we have to stop reading about it, and just do it. Like Jacob and David, we decide to run toward our battle and face it rather than run away from it. We trust that God is with us, and because of that, we won't fail.

Through the Finish Line

There are only a few defining moments, but deciding moments happen hundreds of times a day.

Commitment can be compared to a race. Our initial decision to act on our dreams is like stepping up to the starting line and putting our feet in the blocks. Once the gun goes off, we start running down the track. In some ways, every step we take is a decision we have to make. Maybe we weren't in great physical shape and now our feet, our legs, and even our lungs hurt. With every step we wonder if it's worth it or if we should just stop.

One of the things that I thought about during the week of my brother's funeral was the difference between the defining moments and the deciding moments in life. There are only a few defining moments, but deciding

CHAPTER 7: COMMITMENT

moments happen hundreds of times a day. They happen when we decide to get up off the couch and go for a walk instead of spending another minute in front of the TV, or when we decide to stop procrastinating and take steps toward our dreams. Making a commitment isn't a one-time decision. It's the beginning of a series of deciding moments when we continue making the same decision over and over until our dreams become reality.

In a race, no one really cares how much time we spent practicing, how great we look in our shorts and sneakers, or how well we came off the starting line. The only thing that really counts is if and when we cross the finish line.

Anyone who has seen the movie *Chariots of Fire* will probably remember that Eric Liddell had an odd way of running. When he gave it his all, his head would tilt back so much that he wouldn't be able to see the track.

There's a scene in the movie where Liddell gets knocked down during a race. By the time he gets back on his feet, the rest of the runners are way out in front of him. He stands up full of determination and starts running. As he catches up to the other runners, his head tilts back and he runs with all his might and all his heart. He passes all the other runners, crosses the finish line, and collapses in exhaustion. It wasn't pretty, but through sheer determination and commitment he had not only finished the race, but he had also won it.

I'm not a runner, but I have learned some similar lessons through golf. For example, for a good golf swing, the first key is keep your head level, not down as most people think, until after hitting the ball. And the best way to get the most distance is to hit through the ball, not just to it. In other words, the clubhead should still be speeding up as it gets to and goes "through" the ball.

Also, there's nothing magical about the follow-through. The ball doesn't care what we look like after we've sent it on its merry way. But we can hurt ourselves if we don't allow our body to slow down and come to a balanced finish.

TV commentators often say that a shot or putt was tentative. What they mean is that the golfer hadn't really committed to the shot; the result is usually bad. The shot went off course, or the putt was on the correct line to the hole but stopped short. Regardless of why the golfer was tentative, it ends up ruining his score. For professionals, a bad score can be the difference between making a lot of money and going home empty-handed.

When we decide to go for our dreams, it's important that we have the resolve not only to keep a level head throughout the whole process, but also to be sure that we don't stop short.

Being tentative comes from being unwilling to commit or to make a decision that says, "I choose this and this is what I'm sticking with until I'm finished." From start to finish, each deciding moment is an opportunity to stand in faith and to continue to put our heart into what we're doing, so that we finish well. We need to be like the acorn, knowing what we want to become and changing our minds slowly, if at all.

Taking Action

One of the simplest things we can do to become better decision makers is to simply start making decisions more quickly. Rather than looking over the menu at a restaurant for twenty minutes, simply take a quick look, make a decision, and stick with it. There will be times when we'll regret it, but honing our decision-making skills will improve our lives; having to suffer through a couple of bad meals will be well worth it.

We also need to recognize that many decisions aren't simple choices that can be made at one moment in time. In other words, there is actually a decision process where many small decisions are made over a period of time until the final decision has to be reached. The smaller decisions are nothing more than deciding to continue with the process and gather the next set of facts. In other words, they should be pretty easy, nonstressful, decisions.

An example of a decision process would be applying for a job. The first decision would be to send in an application. Assuming that the company has some interest in hiring the candidate, the next decision might be to go for an interview. During the interview process both parties have a chance to decide if they want to go to the next step. The next step for the

> *People who become very successful have learned how to quickly gather the facts they need and then make a decision. They tend to make decisions quickly and change their minds slowly.*

company would be to make an offer, while the candidate has to decide if this really is the place where he would enjoy working. If the company makes an offer, then the candidate needs to make a final decision about the job. The whole process could take hours, days, or even weeks before the actual "decision" would have to be made.

In other words, sending in an application isn't making a decision to take the job. It's just the start of a series of small decisions we'll make as we gather all the facts. The real decision comes later, once we know all the pros and cons.

Some people simplify their decision making by having automatic guidelines for certain things, such as wearing and actually thinking about the WWJD (What Would Jesus Do) bracelets.

For those people, some decisions are already made. They know in advance what they want to do, so there's no need to gather many facts or think much about choices; the answer is an automatic yes to things that they know Jesus would do. They don't have to wonder if they should be loving and forgiving. The decision is already made: they will be.

People who become very successful have learned how to quickly gather the facts they need and then make a decision. They tend to make decisions quickly and change their minds slowly. People who struggle in life tend to make decisions slowly and change their minds quickly and often. They're like the acorn that can't decide what kind of tree it wants to be, and consequently they never grow.

CHAPTER 8

Courage – Facing Our Fears

Chapter 8

Courage — Facing Our Fears

Then David said to Saul, "Let no man's heart fail because of him; your servant will go and fight with this Philistine."
~ 1 Samuel 17:32

When I was about ten or eleven years old, I spent a typical summer in Maine with friends hanging out at the pool, doing a little caddying on the golf course, finding golf balls in the woods and selling them, lying on our backs and looking at the stars at night, and getting eaten alive by mosquitoes. I'm not sure, but I think that the mosquito is the Maine state bird, although I have heard that Alaska is trying to claim it as theirs.

One day I mentioned that I had never fallen out of a boat. My so-called friend was quick to point out, "There's a first time for everything." Who did this wise guy think he was, a prophet? I was not going to fall out of a boat, and that's all there was to it.

On one particularly nice day we had stopped off at the snack bar for some ice cream and then headed down to the dock to go out in someone's boat. I wasn't using my head as I climbed into the dinghy, because I should have realized that it was a bad idea to climb in on the side of the boat where all the other kids were. But hey, I was a kid and we were in a hurry. The boat tipped the instant I put my foot on the rail, and splash! I was underwater.

I remember thinking, "No problem. I'll be back on the surface in a jiffy." All of a sudden, clunk! My head hit the underside of the dock. I started searching for the edge of the dock, but I couldn't find it. Now panic began to set in. I was just a kid, so there wasn't much of a life that could flash before my eyes. My mind was soon full of thoughts about not finding the edge and running out of air.

It seemed like a long time before my fingers wrapped around the bottom of the dock. I pulled myself to the edge, then reached up on top of the dock, and pulled myself far enough out of the water so that my head and arms were resting on the dock. I gasped for air and cried out to John, the harbormaster, who came running to my aid and pulled me out of the water. I looked over, and there in my left hand was my chocolate ice cream cone.

Fear can cause us to do funny things.

Chocolate *is* my favorite flavor, but it seems odd that while I thought I was fighting for my life, I was holding on to something completely useless. The ice cream wouldn't be any good after being in the salt water, and it was a lousy flotation device. As I dripped all the way home, we all had a pretty good laugh about how scared I'd been, my very soggy chocolate ice cream cone, and that in this case, there really was a "first time for everything."

Fear can cause us to do funny things. At times I've been paralyzed by fear, with every muscle in my body wound so

Chapter 8: COURAGE

tightly that I could hardly breathe. At other times I did stupid stuff, like holding on to an ice cream cone when I thought I was going to drown.

When Goliath defied the armies of Israel, all the battle-tested warriors cowered before him in fear. For forty days Goliath marched out in front of them, taunting and challenging them to send out someone to fight with him. All the soldiers must have been extremely scared, because they ended up putting their futures into the hands of a kid named David.

It must have been particularly hard for Eliab to listen to his little brother David boldly say that he would defeat Goliath. After all, Eliab had just spent forty days being afraid of him. Maybe part of the reason he was so harsh with David was that he was embarrassed about having acted like a coward and that his kid brother had the courage to face this giant.

I took an inventory of my life one day. I asked myself if there was some explanation for why I hadn't taken action on some of my dreams. I thought about events in my past, from my childhood all the way up to the present. Looking back through my life, a certain pattern began to emerge that I really didn't like.

I remembered taking cello lessons in the third grade. The cello is still one of my favorite instruments, and I wish I had continued the lessons. The reason that I quit was really pretty silly. My teacher explained to me that I had two strings that were identical, so I needed to replace one of them with the correct string. The cello was rented from a local music store, so it would have been a simple problem to solve, but I chickened out. I was afraid to talk to the store employees and have them fix the cello. Instead, I stopped taking lessons.

Fast-forward a few years to my junior year in high school when I was taking English-style horseback riding lessons. We'd been doing it for a few weeks, and I was starting to get the hang of it. Then the fateful day came when we were supposed to start jumping over things. Well, that was the end of it for me. I was not going to risk my life and start jumping over fences on the back of some horse, so I quit, which was another decision that I now regret.

The pattern became pretty obvious. In each of these situations and several other instances that I remembered, I would come face to face with something that scared me. I don't consider myself a coward, but I apparently let fear make some decisions for me that I now regret. In his audio program entitled *More Luck*, Charles Burke talks about realizing that he'd never actually failed at anything. He had always quit long before he got to the point where he could fail, or succeed. The pattern in my life was the same. Whenever fear raised its ugly head, I would quit.

Jack Zufelt, author of the best-selling book *The DNA of Success*, says that most people only accomplish two out of every ten goals they set. The reason is probably that those two goals are the ones that are most important to them. They are the goals that they feel they have to reach, and therefore they are willing to make a commitment and take action on them.

Chapter 8: COURAGE

When looking back, I also found times like our move to Germany-times when I had done things that were uncomfortable, even things that scared me, but I didn't quit. I began to wonder what made the difference. Why did I allow fear to ruin something for me in one circumstance, while in another, even scarier circumstance, I had taken action and gotten what I wanted? As Jack Zufelt said, the goals we accomplish are the ones that are really important to us. In other words, they're the ones we really want. If it's possible for us to find the courage to go for our dreams simply by wanting them enough, the question becomes: How do we intensify our desire for them?

Earlier I talked about the process, the price, and the prize, and that many people don't take action on their dreams because the process looks like it will take too long or the price appears to be too high. Where we focus our attention becomes very important. Putting our attention on the prize and keeping our mind on it to the point where we can imagine the joy we will feel when we finally have it will increase our desire. Most of us have heard that the grass is always greener on the other side of the fence. There is often a lot of truth to that statement, especially when we realize that we're neglecting our grass, while the grass on the other side of the fence is getting all the attention.

I teach a noncredit adult education class at a community college. One of the first exercises in the class

> *When we picture the fulfillment of our goals or dreams in the future, we should take time to imagine ourselves actually enjoying how that feels.*

is for the students to finish this sentence: "If I had all the time in the world and all the money I needed, I would . . ." The workbook has space for twelve answers. I offer to give additional paper to anyone who wants it, but so far no one has asked for more. Some people have a hard time thinking of more than one or two things that they would do if their money worries were over.

When it looks like everyone is finished, I go around the room and ask people what they wrote down. In one class, a guy said that if he didn't have to worry about money, he would drive the little car at the driving range that picks up the golf balls. Most of the answers are things like travel, giving to charity, buying a home, paying for the kids' college, or spending more time on a hobby. If people say that they'd like to travel, I ask them where they want to go. A lot of people reply, "Oh, it doesn't matter; I just want to travel."

I explain that it's hard to get emotionally involved with a goal that simply says "travel." It's important that we take time to imagine something clearly enough that we can get excited about actually having it. When we don't care about the goal enough to know exactly what it is, it's unlikely that we will be willing to risk much in order to get it. Instead we get caught up in short-term pleasures and distractions. If the image in our minds of sitting down in front of the tube for some relaxation tonight is stronger than our distant dreams, the TV will win the battle for our attention every time.

Sometimes the fear we face is how we think we might feel if our goals don't become a reality. Because we're afraid that we might end up feeling sad or getting depressed, we decide to just stay where we are. We may not like what we're doing; we may even hate it, but at least it's familiar. We may even be depressed right now, but at least we're used to this particular depression.

When we picture the fulfillment of our goals or dreams in the future, we should take time to imagine ourselves actually enjoying how that feels. We shouldn't let the fear that we might not be happy with our goals or dreams convince us that we're better off unhappy and depressed in our current rut.

There's no guarantee that we will be happier when we reach our goals, but that's not why we're trying to achieve them. As Jim Rohn says, "The major reason for setting a goal is for what it makes of you to accomplish it. What it makes of you will always be the far greater value than what you get."[1] We set and achieve goals so that we will grow and change and become all that God wants us to be.

As Abraham Lincoln pointed out, "Most folks are as happy as they make up their minds to be." Happiness is a decision we make, apart from our circumstances. If we think that we have to have something or that we need to reach some particular point in our lives before we can be happy, chances are good that we'll never be happy.

When looking at my life, I thought that I had found a major problem that had been stopping me. I thought that I was afraid of failure. But then I realized that if I really were afraid of failure, I would probably be a lot more successful in life. It wasn't failure that was scaring me; it was the idea of something being different in my life. I was really just afraid of change, even if that change would make my life better. I was probably more afraid of things going well and of being successful than I was that things wouldn't work out.

Several years ago I was involved in a year-long management training program at work. In one of the classes, the instructor told us that many people procrastinate because they're afraid of the increased responsibility of being promoted. In some ways I'm like that, because I worry about not being able to handle the additional pressure. In my mind, it seemed that it would be better to fail at the old level than to move forward and fail at a higher level. Perhaps it was the fear of having more to lose or simply being afraid I wouldn't be able to handle the new responsibilities.

People who fear success will unconsciously do things that keep them from making progress in their lives. They neglect to do things, sabotaging their own efforts, so that they can stay where they are in their current comfort zone. As I said, fear can make us do funny things. We'll even hold on to something we don't want because we're afraid of losing something we don't even have.

Fear Versus Faith

Fear comes as a result of believing in something that isn't true.

Fear and faith are opposite ends of a scale. Both of them are beliefs in something that hasn't yet happened. Fear comes as a result of believing in something that isn't true. In other words, it comes from believing in a lie, and I call that unbelief. Faith comes from believing the truth.

Some people seem to believe that negative thinking is truer than positive thinking. When it comes right down to it, all our thinking is based on what we believe. It could be untruth, truth, or a mixture of the two. It could be on the fear end of the scale or the faith end of it, though most often it's somewhere in the middle, leaning to one side or the other.

In Mark 11:22-24, Jesus says, "Have faith in God. For assuredly, I say to you, whoever says to this mountain, 'Be removed and be cast into the sea,' and does not doubt in his heart, but believes that those things he says will be done, he will have whatever he says. Therefore I say to you, whatever things you ask when you pray, believe that you receive them, and you will have them." We often believe that the problem is a lack of faith, when in fact it's an abundance of doubts. Our hearts are full of unbelief and fear, so our minds end up full of doubts. William Shakespeare said, "Our doubts are traitors, and make us lose the good we might oft win by fearing to attempt."

As we get a clear picture of our goals and dreams, it's likely that our fears will begin to show up. It's important that we not run from them. Instead it can be very helpful to sit down with a pen and paper and write them down. What is it that we're afraid of? We need to be specific, clearly describing what we fear. A generic fear like "Things might go wrong" isn't good enough. If that were the fear, the next question would be: What things? Then we should make a list with as many things as come to mind. The better we can describe our fears, the easier it will be to confront them. If we have more than one fear, then we need to write them all down.

Next, we need to go through the fears one by one. Just like we dealt with criticism, we need to ask ourselves what's true about our fear and what's not. Are we just making assumptions with no real facts? Or is there some truth to the fear? It could be a warning, telling us about something we need to try to avoid. In cases like that, our caution can help us become more successful.

It can also be very helpful to talk with people who have accomplished something similar to what we want to do. They may have a unique perspective on the issues and fears we're facing. They can shed light on our fears that will help us overcome them.

Chances are good that some of our fears are based on lies. The unbelief that is in our hearts is coming to the surface, and we need to confront it with God's truth. The lie could be something as simple as not being convinced that God loves us. We're afraid because we think that He will punish us for some past sin, that we're not worthy of His love, and He will refuse to help us when we cry out to Him. This is when it becomes extremely important to memorize and meditate on scriptures that tell us about God's love. First John 4:18 tells us that there is no fear in love, because perfect love "casts out" fear.

In Ephesians 3:14-21 the apostle Paul prayed that all of us would be firmly grounded in God's love and that we would be able to comprehend just how much God loves us. When we are convinced that God loves us more than we can imagine, we become like the righteous in Proverbs 28:1, and we will have the boldness and courage of a lion.

Today Versus Tomorrow

Jesus tells us, "Therefore do not worry about tomorrow, for tomorrow will worry about its own things. Sufficient for the day is its own trouble" (Matt. 6:34). It can be very easy to get so caught up in thinking about what could go wrong tomorrow that we either fail to take action today or we're distracted by our worries and we don't do a good job. We need to concentrate on what's happening right now and stop thinking about what might happen later.

When David prepared for his battle with Goliath, the questions that he was dealing with were things like "Does this armor help me, or just get in my way? How many stones should I take with me?" He hadn't even thought far enough ahead to realize that he would need a sword if he was going to cut off Goliath's head. I'm sure that he wasn't worrying whether the king's daughter was good-looking or if they would have good weather for the wedding. He was looking at the battle and no further.

We can learn some things about life by comparing a round of golf to reaching a goal or realizing a dream. The golfer who starts worrying about his final score or the putt he might have to make on number eleven before he even hits his first shot on the first hole will waste a lot of energy worrying about the future. He won't concentrate on the shot he's getting ready to make, and he could end up with a poor result.

> *Our thoughts, feelings, and actions are determined by our beliefs.*

Most amateur golfers will gladly spend money on a new golf club or practice for hours at the driving range in the hope that they will improve their swing and lower their score.

One day I told a friend and fellow golfer that I would really like to have a swing like Ernie Els. Ernie is known for the smooth tempo and seemingly effortless power of his golf swing. My friend remarked that he'd rather have a lower score. I realized he was right: there's no place on the scorecard to describe my swing; there's only a small box for recording my score. Three really ugly shots and a lucky putt still add up to par on a par four, and that's a good score. As someone once said, "They don't ask how, they just ask how many."

When facing a shot near water, a lot of golfers will start to worry and tell themselves, "Don't go in the water. Don't go in the water." They step up to the ball, take a whack at it, and splash! The ball goes into the water, and they exclaim, "I knew I was going to do that! I always go in the water on this hole!"

Regardless of how hard they tried to talk themselves out of putting the ball in the water, the picture that was in their minds was of the ball going in the water. What they should be saying to themselves is something positive that creates the picture of what they want rather than what they don't want: "I will put this shot in the fairway."

Golfers have no control over many other factors that influence the results, such as the weather and the condition of the golf course. Having a positive image is no guarantee that they'll hit a good shot, and there will be times when they are thinking negatively but the ball lands in the fairway in spite of it.

The greatest influence on the golfers' performance isn't what they are saying to themselves; it's what they really believe. Even with a positive picture, their minds may still be full of doubts caused by the times in the past when things didn't work out as well as they had hoped. The battle between fear and faith will begin, and the result will be influenced most by whichever one wins.

So it becomes much more imperative that they choose to keep a positive mental image and attitude. Fear will be flashing images of them messing up the shot, and the ball going in the water. Faith, on the other hand, will be presenting them with images of the ball landing in the fairway. The question becomes: Which belief will be stronger at the moment they hit the ball?

Our thoughts, feelings, and actions are determined by our beliefs. The lie detector relies on subtle changes that take place in our bodies when we know that we're lying. Some people have become so adept at lying that they can control their physical reactions, but most people's brains will register the conflict and cause a physical response.

For golfers it means that their palms will get sweaty if they write down a five, when their actual score was six. Worry and negative thoughts will create subtle changes in how they perform. If they are picturing the ball going into the water, even if they're saying something different, their brains will send signals to their muscles, and the unconscious physical response will be to do something to hit the ball toward the water.

Simply saying all the right things and maybe even praying great prayers won't do as much good if the hope in our minds is clouded by negative images, fears, and doubts. When it comes to our faith and overcoming our fears, it's essential to create positive mental images and combine them with positive emotions.

In Philippians 4:6-8 the apostle Paul explains the steps we should follow. First he tells us not to worry about anything. Instead we should bring all our requests to God. Beyond just offering up a laundry list of wants and needs, we should offer thanks, in advance, for the answers that God will give us. The promise is that God's peace will then guard our hearts and minds. In other words, God's peace will rule our emotions and thoughts. He then tells us to take control of our thoughts and even gives us a list of things that we should think about — positive things like truth and justice.

Controlling our minds can be hard work, especially if we simply try to prevent negative, fearful, or worrisome thoughts. The answer, as Paul points out, isn't to try to stop the negative thoughts. Instead we should fill our minds with things that are true, beautiful, and positive. As D. Martin Lloyd-Jones put it, "Have you realized that most of your unhappiness in life is due to the fact that you are listening to yourself instead of talking to yourself?" When we listen to ourselves, the unbelief that is in our hearts fills our thinking. The result can be everything from unhappiness to fear and even disobedience toward God.

Chapter 8: COURAGE

As David walked out onto the field to face Goliath, I'm sure that he carefully chose his thoughts. He might have reminded himself of the times he had easily hit small targets with his sling, and Goliath was huge, so there was no way he could miss.

He probably thought about the times when God delivered him from the lion and the bear. And I'm sure he remembered God's promise to give His people victory over their enemies.

Perhaps he even mentally rehearsed how he would take a stone, put it in the sling, and hit Goliath right in the middle of his forehead. Maybe he even imagined the small thud of the stone hitting its target and the loud thud of Goliath hitting the ground. The more complete the image, the better.

If fear came up in his heart, I'm sure he quickly silenced it, controlling his thoughts by thinking about God's power and faithfulness. He decided to put his complete confidence in what God would do. David could have courage in spite of the odds being against him, because he knew that God loved him, and that God would not fail him.

> *But we know that God is the source of all we will ever need and He will make sure that we reap the benefits of the seeds, the energy we've sown through our thoughts and actions, as long as we don't lose heart, as long as we remain courageous and continue to sow.*

Sowing Seeds

Farmers are very familiar with all the problems that can come up during a summer. It could be too dry or there might be too much rain. There are many things that they can't control, and in some cases, all that they own is riding on the result. They have to be willing to accept the risk and sow their seeds in faith, or they will never be able to reap the harvest.

In Luke 6:38 Jesus says, "Give, and it will be given to you: good measure, pressed down, shaken together, and running over will be put into your bosom. For with the same measure that you use, it will be measured back to you." Galatians 6:7 tells us, "Do not be deceived, God is not mocked; for whatever a man sows, that he will also reap."

I mentioned earlier that God's way of doing things is usually the opposite of how the world thinks things should be done. While most people are trying to take all they can get and are anxiously clutching all that they have, we need to learn how to give. In God's kingdom, the only way to get anything is by giving. We can't expect to reap if we haven't been willing to step out in faith, take some risks, and give.

It takes a lot of courage to get up every day and give of our time, energy, and money. It's even more difficult when other people tell us that we're making a mistake, that we should be putting ourselves first and taking all we can while we have the chance. But while most people are working in vain to get more while doing less, we realize that God is the one who rewards us. He sees what we're doing, and we have the faith and therefore the courage to continue giving even if we don't get quick results.

Ecclesiastes 11:4-6 says, "He who observes the wind will not sow, and he who regards the clouds will not reap. As you do not know what is the way of the wind, or how the bones grow in the womb of her who is with child, so you do not know the works of God who makes everything. In the morning sow your seed, and in the evening do not withhold your hand; for you do not know which will prosper, either this or that, or whether both alike will be good."

People who don't sow their seed but worry about what might go wrong don't understand that everything comes from God. What God expects from us is that we will give, and continue to give, regardless of the circumstances. He wants us to continue in faith until the seeds we've planted begin to grow and bear fruit. We understand that our desires and goals will require that we put forth the energy consistently and continually, sowing in the morning and the evening, and that we will need patience as we allow God to bring our efforts to fruition in His time.

Just like the farmer who plants his seeds, we know that there is no such thing as immediate fruit. Even fast food has ingredients that had to grow over time. We may get our Happy Meal within minutes, but the cow in the burger, the wheat in the bun, and the potatoes in our french fries all took months to grow. Galatians 6:9 reminds us, "And let us not grow weary while doing good, for in due season we shall reap if we do not lose heart."

It takes courage to face the risk of failure, to continue to hold our dreams steadfast in our minds, and to remain firm in our faith as we wait through all the ups and downs for our harvest. But we know that God is the source of all we will ever need and that He will make sure that we reap the benefits of the seeds, the energy we've sown through our thoughts and actions, as long as we don't lose heart and as long as we remain courageous and continue to sow.

Taking Action

Fear comes from two main sources: negative images and lack of knowledge.

> *When we know what the outcome will be, we don't have to worry about all the negative possibilities. When we know that we can't lose, we'll have the courage to play the game.*

Some of our fears come from the negative images that we have in our minds — the bad things that we think might happen to us. These images are based on our memories and beliefs about the pain and embarrassment we have felt or might feel when things don't go as we planned.

We need to create positive mental images of how we will feel once we've reached our goals or fulfilled our dreams. In order for those images, rather than the negative images of failure, to come up when we think about our goals, we need to consistently sow the positive images in our minds over and over.

The scientists at NASA once tried an experiment. They had some volunteer astronauts wear goggles that turned everything they saw upside down. What they were trying to determine was how people would react to being disoriented over a long period of time, which is similar to prolonged weightlessness. What happened took them completely by surprise.

Depending on the individual, at some point after having worn the goggles for twenty-seven to thirty days, all of the volunteers had a shift in their brains and what they saw suddenly turned right side up again. They learned that the human brain is a lot more flexible than they thought, and that even something as ingrained as how we physically see the world can be changed if we will just stick with the new way of viewing the world consistently and for a long enough time.

For the next thirty days, make a commitment to spend time visualizing yourself enjoying the achievement of your goal. When you do your visualization be sure to put a big smile on your face. Do this four to five times a day, every day, for at least five minutes at a time. It will take about twenty to twenty-five minutes each day, but you should look at this as sowing your seed in the morning and evening. It will prosper and bear the fruit: a positive image will be associated with your goal, and your motivation for reaching that goal will soar.

You might find it hard to see yourself achieving your goal. Stacy Mayo, author of I *Can't Believe* I *Get PAID To Do This*, says, "If this is the case, you might want to try visualizing yourself accomplishing one small step toward your dream rather than achieving the whole thing."[2] Whatever your goal is you will reach it one step at a time. Having the courage to take each step along the way will help you develop the confidence to reach even the largest goal.

The other source of our fears is a lack of knowledge or understanding. Walking around in the dark in an unfamiliar room makes us afraid, but when we turn on the light, and can see what we're dealing with, the fear will go away. When we know what the outcome will be, we don't have to worry about all the negative possibilities. When we know that we can't lose, we'll have the courage to play the game.

Jesus tells us, "Do not fear, little flock, for it is your Father's good pleasure to give you the kingdom" (Luke 12:32). As I've already discussed, the only way for us to fail is if we listen to our fears and refuse to take action. God wants us to be successful. He has given us the gifts and abilities we need, and He will make sure that we get good results, if we will seek Him first and trust Him.

Take some time to memorize and meditate on Luke 12:32. Another good Scripture is Ephesians 3:20-21. In those verses we learn that God has placed the power in all of us that allows Him to do exceedingly abundantly beyond what we can imagine. That power is in the seeds of our faith, which we sow as we think and act in accordance with our hope.

CHAPTER 9

Celebration – Rejoicing in Achievement

Chapter 9

Celebration – Rejoicing in Achievement

> Now it had happened as they were coming home, when David was returning from the slaughter of the Philistine, that the women had come out of all the cities of Israel, singing and dancing, to meet King Saul, with tambourines, with joy, and with musical instruments. So the women sang as they danced, and said:
>
> "Saul has slain his thousands,
> And David his ten thousands."
>
> ~ 1 Samuel 18:6–7

It was the fourth patch I had sent to this customer, and the problem was still there. I was working as a software support engineer for a large computer manufacturer, and my job was to find and fix bugs in their software. Some aspects of the job were very interesting. I often felt like a detective arriving at the scene of a crime and trying to figure out what happened — sort of a computer nerd's version of a whodunit.

In this case, the customer was seeing a particular symptom that

> *We start to focus so much on what we still have to do, that we don't acknowledge ourselves for the progress we're making. Our life can begin to feel like a line from a Robert Frost poem that says, "But I have promises to keep, and miles to go before I sleep, and miles to go before I sleep."*

was making it hard for him to get his work done. The hours I had spent searching for the problem probably added up to several weeks' worth of time. I'd modified the software so that I could keep track of what was going on, and I ran test after test, some of them taking days.

I had found and fixed four problems that would cause the symptom this customer was seeing, but I still hadn't found the exact problem he was having. I understood why he was getting upset. I had been working on this problem for him for almost a year, and we didn't appear to be any closer to fixing it.

I made some further changes to my modifications so that we could track what was happening for a longer period of time, and I ran my tests again. This time I found a problem in an area of the software that I hadn't looked at before. I wrote a fix and sent it to the customer. I got a short reply from him saying that the problem was now fixed, and he thanked me. I breathed a sigh of relief and immediately got back to work on the other problems I was investigating.

Working in software support can be a strange job. The constant interruptions and changing priorities can drive some people crazy. For me it was like working in an emergency room, where doctors rarely see the same patient twice and are always dealing with new problems. I enjoyed it.

When we lived in Germany, I had the opportunity to move from Stuttgart to the former East Germany shortly after the wall that had separated East from West Germany had been taken down. I felt that God was leading us to go, so I applied for and got a position in Dresden. My boss in

Chapter 9: CELEBRATION

Stuttgart put an ad in the local newspaper, and we started interviewing candidates to replace me.

One of the guys I interviewed was a typical programmer. By that I mean that he had always worked on one project at a time, usually for several months in a row. During the interview, I decided to describe my typical day to him. It went something like this: I would be working on six or seven different problems at a time, talking on the phone with an irate customer, and there would be two or three hardware engineers standing in line waiting to ask me questions. The job consisted of dealing with one angry customer after another, each with a critical problem, day after day. The guy I was interviewing looked at me and said, "I don't want to do that!" I told him that the job probably wouldn't be a good fit for him.

One of the problems with working in software support is that it can be a thankless job. Technicians work long hours to fix problems, send solutions off to the customers, and then never hear from them again. It's perfectly understandable. The bottom line was that they had been dealing with problems, and they were just glad the problems were fixed. All the customers wanted to do was get back to work, and taking time to thank someone for fixing their problems, especially those they felt they should not have had to deal with — was the last thing on their mind.

Working on our goals can become a thankless job as well. When we have large goals that will take a lot of time and energy to achieve, it can be easy for us to lose sight of the importance of appreciating our own efforts. We start to focus so much on what we still have to do, that we don't acknowledge ourselves for the progress we're making. Our lives can begin to feel like the line from a Robert Frost poem that says, "But I have promises to keep, and miles to go before I sleep, and miles to go before I sleep."

Second Timothy 2:6 says, "The hardworking farmer must be first to partake of the crops." If farmers never got to enjoy the harvest, it wouldn't take long before they would quit doing all the work, and we're no different. We have to know that we will receive some reward for the work we're doing.

> *People celebrate things in their own ways. Some people make a big deal about things that may seem insignificant to others, while other people don't get excited about anything.*

With things that will take a while before all the work is finished, such as achieving a large goal or realizing a long-standing dream, it's important that we recognize the milestones we pass along the way. It may be as simple as looking back on a day's accomplishments, stopping for a moment to take a deep breath, and being thankful and rejoicing in the steps we've taken.

I used to work with a group that developed a series of business seminars and workshops. One of the main concepts that they taught was that we become successful the minute we start taking steps toward the achievement of our goals. In other words, we don't become successful when we reach the goal; we are already successful the moment we start and continue to work on it.

Chapter 9: CELEBRATION

They also taught that it's important to take our large goals and break them down into smaller, more manageable tasks. One of the advantages is that this helps us see when we're making measurable progress on our goals. It will be easier for us to stay motivated as we check off each task because we'll know that we're that much closer to the completion of our goals.

The other advantage is that a large goal will be less daunting when we see that it's really just made up of a series of smaller, more easily achievable steps. It's like the Chinese proverb about the journey of a thousand miles starting with just one step. We don't have to take one big thousand-mile leap. Reaching any goal, no matter how big, is just a matter of taking one step after another, and before we know it, we will have reached our destination.

In 1 Samuel 18 we read about the celebration that came after David killed Goliath. It was a major victory for the nation of Israel and for David. I like to think that David was well aware that there would be many battles on his road to becoming king. Defeating Goliath was a big step in that process, and it was time to really celebrate. This was a victory that he would remember for the rest of his life.

One of the things that I admire about David was that he wrote about his experiences. He used his writing to not only keep a record of all his trials and triumphs, but also to help him praise and worship God no matter what struggles he faced. As he wrote, he would remind himself of God's goodness and blessings. Everything he struggled through was offered up in prayer, and all that he accomplished was turned into praise.

Great Blessings

I can't remember exactly where I heard this, but I believe it was in a movie I saw. One of the characters was talking about the difference between Italian and English men. He said that when an Italian man's son would return home, he would hug him, kiss him, and weep for joy, even if the son had only been gone for the weekend. When the Englishman would greet his son, they would simply shake hands and exchange pleasantries, even if the son had been away for months.

People celebrate things in their own ways. Some people make a big deal about things that may seem insignificant to others, while other people don't get excited about anything. Proverbs 14:10 says, "The heart knows its own bitterness, and a stranger does not share its joy." How we each feel about what happens in our lives is as unique as our fingerprints. The emotions we experience are a combination of the memories we have of similar situations in our past and our beliefs about ourselves. No one else will ever be able to fully understand what we feel, and many times it's hard for us to completely understand it.

There is a story in 2 Samuel 6 about David bringing the ark of God into the city of Jerusalem. Through a series of events, the ark had ended up at the house of Obed-Edom, and God had been blessing him because of it. But now David was bringing the ark into the city, and he was so excited that he danced before the Lord with all his might. In verse 16 we read that David's wife Michal, Saul's daughter, saw him leaping and whirling around and that she despised him because of it.

Chapter 9: CELEBRATION

Even if David went way overboard with his dancing, Michal seemed to be missing the whole point. This was an event of mammoth proportions. David wasn't just bringing some artifact to a museum so that it could be put on display. He was bringing the very presence of God into the city. God's blessings would come upon the city, just as they had for Obed-Edom and his house. This was an absolutely incredible event, and David had every right to be excited, even to the point of looking foolish.

Not every event worth celebrating in our lives will be as major as what David experienced when bringing the ark home to Jerusalem. We don't have to go overboard for every little thing. But celebrating is important because through celebration we reward ourselves for what we've done, and reinforce the habits we want to develop.

No matter what else God may want for us, one thing is certain: He wants us to be thankful in all things and at all times.

Deciding on specific, appropriate rewards in advance can help us complete our tasks. It's probably not appropriate to reward ourselves for sticking to our diet at lunch by eating a whole bag of cookies for dinner, but when we achieve a goal or reach a milestone on the way to one of our goals, we might decide to go to dinner or a movie.

We should plan something really big, like that vacation we've always wanted to take, when we achieve one of our major goals.

Knowing how we will celebrate can help us increase the intensity of our desire to reach our goals. As we imagine celebrating, we should allow ourselves to experience all the joy and satisfaction we will feel when we accomplish our goal. It will take some effort and discipline to keep that image and those good emotions in the forefront of our minds when we run into difficulties, but by doing it every day, we will become unstoppable in the pursuit of our dreams.

The Journey

Cervantes once said that the journey is better than the inn. As Earl Nightingale points out, they didn't have Holiday Inns when Cervantes was alive. Today we complain if they have stale bagels at the complimentary breakfast. But in Cervantes's day, the inns were usually dirty and very dangerous. The traveler was likely to get robbed, maybe even murdered, while staying at the inn.

As much as we need to rejoice when we accomplish one of our tasks, and even more when we reach a goal, the fact is that we will spend most of our lives between goals. As I mentioned before, if we're always waiting until we reach some point or we feel that we have to have some particular thing before we can be happy, we'll probably never be happy. Learning to rejoice not only in accomplishment but also in labor is important for our overall happiness and well-being. We can be thankful for the gifts and strength to accomplish our goals as we pursue them.

In an earlier chapter I talked about telling my manager that I hated my job. I felt like I wasn't accomplishing anything, and that my job wasn't using my gifts and abilities. It was very frustrating and I forgot all about God's will. By that I mean the will of God found in 1 Thessalonians 5:18 where it says, "In everything give thanks; for this is the will of God in Christ Jesus for you."

No matter what else God may want for us, one thing is certain: He wants us to be thankful in all things and at all times. Everything we have, even every day that we're alive, is a gift God has given us. One thing I never should have done was to let something like a little frustration with my job become an excuse for me to be ungrateful.

David recognized that God was constantly blessing him. In Psalm 68:19 he wrote, "Blessed be the Lord, who daily loads us with benefits, the God of our salvation!" If I'm not sure that God is loading me with benefits every day, the problem isn't God. It's more likely that I'm taking too many things for granted and that I'm not looking at the miracles in and around me or perhaps that I'm spending too much time complaining about what I don't have rather than being thankful for what do I have.

There are times when God answers my prayers and I act like one of the customers from my software support days. The answer comes and I move on to other things with nothing more than a quick thanks to God, if I remember to be thankful at all. God still loves me, and He understands the problem all too well. But my desire is to develop an attitude of gratitude, to develop the habit of praise and thanksgiving. I want to be more like David, who wasn't simply going through the motions. He worshipped God with all his heart. He was truly thankful for all God had done and for all He promised to do.

Thankful in Advance

Zig Ziglar says that the more thankful we are for what we have, the more we'll have to be thankful for. But as we ask ourselves if we're being thankful for all we have, I think we should also ask if we're fully aware of all that God has already given us. For example, one of the secrets for living in abundance is recognizing and being thankful that abundance is already ours.

In other words, it isn't something we'll have later (for example, when we have a million dollars or get to heaven); it's something we have right now, by faith. What that means is we will see it in our lives after we start and continue to act and speak in a manner that says, "I have abundance in Christ."

For the next week (well, really for the rest of our lives, but we'll start with seven days), stop all complaining.

In Philippians 4:6, Paul tells us that we should make our requests known to God "with thanksgiving." Since faith is the substance of things we hope for — in other words, being fully convinced that we already have something before we can physically touch it — then part of faith is being thankful for the answer at the time we make the request. When we expect what we ask for and are already truly thankful for it, that's faith at work.

Chapter 9: CELEBRATION

In 2 Chronicles 20 is a well-known story about a king named Jehoshaphat. A large army was coming to invade Jehoshaphat's kingdom. There was no way that he would be able to defeat this army, so he did what most of us would have done: he became very scared and cried out to God. As Jehoshaphat and the people who were with him prayed, God spoke and told them not to be afraid because He would fight the battle for them.

There are two things that I really love about this story. The first one is the end of Jehoshaphat's prayer in 2 Chronicles 20:12, where he says, "O our God, will You not judge them? For we have no power against this great multitude that is coming against us; nor do we know what to do, but our eyes are upon You." In this prayer he does some things that we need to do when we're facing very difficult situations. We need to recognize our own weaknesses and the fact that we probably don't even know what to do, and then we need to look to God. God will give us all that we need to overcome any circumstances we face. All we have to do is seek Him first.

The other thing that I love is how they marched out to the battle the next morning. Verse 21 says that they believed God and put the singers out in front of the soldiers. As a singer, I imagine that it would have been very intimidating to be in front of the soldiers as everyone marched into battle. But in verses 22-25 we read that the minute they started singing and praising God, God caused the invading army to start fighting against each other. By the time Jehoshaphat and his people got there, everyone was dead.

It goes on to say that they spent the next three days collecting the "abundance of valuables" that they found among the dead bodies.

Because they looked to God, believed His promise to them, and began thanking Him in advance, they not only won a battle without having to fight, but they also got to enjoy the spoils of war. By trusting in God, they were able to see Him turn a potential disaster into a miraculous victory.

I don't think it's a coincidence that David was someone who worshipped God. He understood that God would take care of his every need, and even when he questioned the things that were happening in his life, he always reminded himself that God had never failed. David's faith was expressed in praise to God not only for who God is or what He had done, but also for all that He was going to do. David knew that God would always fulfill His promises, and he was thankful in advance.

Taking Action

The words that we say tell us a lot about what we believe. If we spend all our time complaining, it might be showing us that our faith in God's blessings and what He can do in our lives is limited. Ephesians 4:29 tells us that we shouldn't allow words that are rotten or worthless to come out of our mouths. Instead, what we say should benefit and encourage others.

Proverbs 18:21 says, "Death and life are in the power of the tongue, and those who love it will eat its fruit." It may be easy to think that what we say doesn't matter all that much, but our words have an effect on everyone who hears them, especially on us. We hear ourselves talk all the time, and the things we say will strengthen the beliefs that we have, so it's important that we choose our words carefully. For the next week (well, really for the rest of our lives, but we'll start with seven days), stop all complaining.

You'll probably find that it will be a struggle, but it can help if you also make sure to avoid spending time with people who complain a lot. If you're in an environment where people are complaining about things, it's too easy to chime in with everyone else. So during this next week, be sure to stay away from negative people as much as possible.

We've talked about a journal a couple of times. For the next thirty days, take time every day to write down ten things for which you're thankful. The list needs to have new things on it every day; it's no fair using the same ten things over and over. The best time to do it is in the morning, but evenings can also work well. The goal is to open your eyes to all that you have for which you can be thankful.

Even a job that I hated paid me well, offered affordable health insurance, paid vacation, a 401K, and many other benefits. When we start thinking about being thankful for everything we have, it will also be easier to stop complaining.

Also, remember what Philippians 4:8 says: "Finally, brethren, whatever things are true, whatever things are noble, whatever things are just, whatever things are pure, whatever things are lovely, whatever things are of good report, if there is any virtue and if there is anything praiseworthy — meditate on these things." And that sounds like good advice to me.

CHAPTER 10

The Conquering Life

Chapter 10

The Conquering Life

The LORD *has sought for Himself a man after His own heart, and the* LORD *has commanded him to be commander over His people . . .* ~ 1 Samuel 13:14

The first time that I ever rode on a roller coaster was my twenty-first birthday, when some friends took me to Elitch Gardens in Denver, Colorado. At the time, they had a large wooden roller coaster. As we stood in line, all I could hear was the sound of the coaster zooming around the track and people screaming at the top of their lungs. That probably should have been warning enough, but my friends assured me it would be fun.

When we finally got through the gate, a crowd of little kids raced on ahead of me. My two friends were able to get in one of the cars, but the other cars filled up before I could climb in, so I waited for the next train. As the next train pulled in, pretty much the same thing happened again, as another rush of kids filled up every car except the last one, so I grabbed the last car and sat down. It was one of those cases where ignorance is bliss, but only for a very short period of time. The bliss started to fade the second they lowered the bar and pinned me into the car.

I distinctly remember how the train slowly headed up the first hill, clicking all the way. I began to see the cars in front of me disappear as the train picked up speed. When I reached the top of the hill, something happened that made me realize that it had probably been a bad idea to sit in the last car of the train on my first-ever roller coaster ride. As I went over the top of the hill, I could feel the car lift off the track, and I had something that I can only refer to as a Wile E. Coyote moment — that moment when a cartoon character runs off the edge of a cliff but doesn't actually start to fall until the painful realization sinks in that he's going down and there's nothing he can do about it.

Off we went at breakneck speed, rounding corners and rushing through tunnels. All I kept thinking was that I was too tall to be on one of these things, and I was sure that I'd be decapitated. I think that the imprint of my fingers is probably still on the bar of that particular car. As I stepped out of the car at the end of the ride, my friends looked very concerned as they asked if I was all right.

> *As I went over the top of the hill, I could feel the car lift off the track, and I had something that I can only refer to as a Wile E. Coyote moment.*

In 1996 my family and I were living near Dresden in the eastern part of Germany. We'd been there for five years, and some changes in my job were causing some real problems. The biggest problem was that I was spending 80 percent of my time on the road. I usually left early on Monday morning and got home late Friday evening. Since I had been at customer sites, hotels, and restaurants all week, my only thought was of staying home on the couch. The

Chapter 10: The Conquering Life

problem was that my wife had been home all week with the kids and she wanted to go out.

The weekends would start with me handing my dirty laundry to my wife, and then we'd get into a really good fight. We didn't have much time together, but over the course of the weekend the laundry would get done and my wife and I would make up. Then it was time for me to pack and leave for another week on the road. It had been going on like that for more than two years, and I was really getting tired of it.

One night I was talking with the engineering support group back in the States, and I innocently asked if they were looking to hire anyone. The guy said that they were and that he'd talk with his manager about me. I went home that evening and broached the subject with my wife. We knew that the kids would be really happy about moving back to the United States, and we felt this might be God opening a door for us not only to return to the States, but also to live in New England, which had been another of my long-standing dreams.

As I started serious discussions with the management about relocating back home, it began to feel similar to climbing that first hill on my first-ever roller coaster ride. When they offered me the job, it was just like we'd crested the hill, then my Wile E. Coyote moment came, and we were off for a wild ride. As everything unfolded, I was probably more scared about it than my wife, and we were both amazed at how God worked out all the details, even helping us find a house the very first day we looked. Things moved so fast that we were back in the United States almost before we knew it, and another dream had come true.

I realized something about following God's will for my life, and perhaps you've had a similar experience. It can seem like it takes forever for things to get started. A lot of preparation is required. God will bring circumstances, struggles, and delays into our lives to begin changing our hearts and testing our faith.

He will carefully lay the groundwork in us and prepare the path before us until the day when everything seems to suddenly fall into place. It's then that we will see that those delays that frustrated us were really God working things according to His perfect timing, and all those struggles have prepared us for the on-going difficulties that are about to come. On that fateful day we will have our Wile E. Coyote moments when we realize that God really is going to open the doors, and we will start moving toward our goals at breakneck speeds.

The struggles aren't over. The roller coaster still has a long way to go. But roller coaster rides and following God's will have something in common. With both of them it's a bad idea to jump out before reaching the end. The safest thing is to hang on and have faith that God will be with us all the way, and we'll make it to the end.

For David, the battle with Goliath must have been a really wild ride, but it was all just part of a process that God was using to prepare David to become king. And David had been preparing as well. He had been meditating on God's word and learning to listen to God's leading. He had worked hard at everything he was given to do. He had not only learned what it was to be faithful, but he had also experienced God's faithfulness. We don't know how aware David was of the process he was going through, but it is clear that he was willing to do whatever God commanded him, even if it meant putting his life on the line. He was able to keep his eye on the prize, even when everyone around him was telling him he was crazy.

David had experienced God's deliverance more than once, and he knew beyond any doubt that God would not fail him. He knew that God would fulfill His promises no matter what obstacles were in the way and no matter how long it would take. His lack of experience as a soldier had worked to his advantage because it forced him to be creative and rely on his strengths to kill Goliath. And when the time came for him to face Goliath, he didn't back down. He was able to be courageous because he knew what God could do. And he knew that it was God, and not David, who deserved all the glory.

David After Goliath

The battle with Goliath forever changed David and the direction of his life. He began to take on more and more leadership within the kingdom, and he fought many battles, but he wasn't king yet. That would take longer, and there would be many struggles, along with disappointment and betrayal, before he would wear the crown and rule God's people.

> But he never would have had that experience of God's provision and power unless he had been willing to do something that was uncomfortable for him.

It would be nice if there were such a thing as one final battle, and then all smooth sailing from there, or if we could somehow muster up enough faith that we'd never have another problem.

If David's life is any indication, what we can look forward to is ongoing problems. Even Jesus promised us that we'd have troubles in this life. But Jesus also told us that we don't have to worry because He has overcome (John 16:33). In the letters to the seven churches in the book of Revelation, a promise is given to those in each church who overcome. It's the overcomers who will receive the greatest blessings.

Not long ago I taught a Sunday school class at our church based on the book by John Ortberg entitled *If You Want to Walk on Water, You've Got to Get out of the Boat*. One of the principles in the class was that the boat represents our comfort zone, and all of us have our "boats." I can't imagine what it must have been like for Peter to walk on the water. But he never would have had that experience of God's provision and power unless he had been willing to do something that was uncomfortable for him. As frightening as it must have been, he had to step out of the boat.

It's possible to get comfortable with a lot of things in life, even some very bad circumstances. But we get so used to them, and they become so familiar, that the thought of getting out of those circumstances scares us.

We can end up like the other eleven disciples who were in the boat on that stormy night. The wind and the waves were tossing the boat around, possibly forcing them to have to continually bail it out, but they held on to the boat for dear life. And in spite of what they might have thought about what Peter did, the safest place that night wasn't in the boat; it was out there with Jesus, walking on the water.

Following God's will for our lives, whether we seem to stumble onto it or He tells us directly, will mean that we have problems. Even after David was king, he still had a lot of problems to deal with. Some of them were things that he brought on himself because he hadn't paid enough attention to his family, and some were the result of sins he committed. But other problems that he faced were simply part of following God's will for his life.

Repentance and Forgiveness

One thing we learned when we lived in Germany is that Germans love to take walks. It's a small country with a lot of people, so the forests tend to have clearly marked paths, with an occasional bench where people can sit and rest.

In some ways, our minds are like forests with paths that take us through our memories and benches where we spend time with our thoughts. No matter what it is, the more often we think about something — especially if there is a lot of emotion combined with our thoughts, the more "clearly marked" that path will become in our minds.

Jesus taught that the battle against sin isn't just in our outward actions. In Matthew 5:21-30 He tells us that murder and adultery actually start with the thoughts that we keep repeating in our minds. In other words, sin is a habitual way of thinking that will express itself in our emotions and actions. In the first few verses of 2

Corinthians 10, Paul reminds us that God has given us powerful spiritual weapons, like His word, that allow us to take control of our thoughts and tear down the strongholds of deeply ingrained beliefs and sin.

Psalm 119:59 describes repentance by saying, "I thought on my ways, and turned my feet to Your testimonies." When I think about how our minds work, I imagine repentance to be like a walk I'm taking through the forest. Rather than following the old familiar path to sin, I make a decision to walk in a different direction. As I continue to do that, the old path becomes overgrown and the bench begins to fall apart from neglect. At first the new path will be harder to find, and it will require more work to follow it. But with time it will become clearer, and I'll build a new bench where I can sit and commune with God.

Repentance and forgiveness were very important in David's life. Long after his battle with Goliath, David lost the battle against his own sin and ended up committing adultery and murder. When the prophet Nathan confronted him, he immediately admitted his sin (2 Sam. 12:13). David wrote about the experience in Psalm 51, where he confessed his sin and asked God to forgive and cleanse him. David understood that sacrifices and offerings were not what God wanted from him. David's heart was broken because of his sin, and that's what was most important to God.

True repentance comes from knowing that God is holy and merciful, recognizing how we have sinned against Him, and then looking to Him for forgiveness. It starts with confession and leads to cleansing and change. As Psalm

119:59 points out, repentance is first and foremost a change of mind that changes our actions.

We all know the saying "forgive and forget." When God forgives us, He chooses to forget our sins (Jer. 31:34). We often struggle with the memories of our sins and have difficulty forgiving ourselves, but God simply makes the decision that He will forget. It's like the paths in the forest; God decides that He will never again go down the path to our sin. He no longer mentions it to us, and as far as He's concerned, it's over.

> *This person's jaw dropped, and he looked at me rather incredulously and asked, "Do you mean that God spoke to you?" I said, "In a voice that shook the house, no. But He did speak to my heart, and I knew what He wanted me to do."*

Unfortunately, I often find myself revisiting old sins and beating myself up because of them. I keep asking God to forgive me again and again. I'm sure that He does, but He may also wonder why I keep going down those old paths when He's promised that He will never go there again. Not only can it be hard for us to accept God's forgiveness for the sins we've committed, but forgiving people who have sinned against us can also be a struggle.

Not long ago I was talking with someone about God's forgiveness, and I told him that God chooses to forget when He forgives us. He really couldn't understand it, because he seemed unable to forgive someone in his life. He insisted that he really wanted to forgive the other person, but he had been deeply hurt and he couldn't stop thinking about it.

In some ways repentance and forgiveness are similar. Whether it's the path to some sin or the memory of how someone hurt us, we must make the decision to take a different path. As long as we allow the old thoughts to occupy our minds, we will continue to follow our old ways. It will take conscious effort to make the changes, to take a new path toward holiness and forgiveness. But as we do, we'll find that the old thoughts will bother us less often and leave us more quickly. We'll find that we can have victory over even the more fortified strongholds, and we'll experience peace.

Knowing God's Will

I was attending Bible college when my wife and I got married. We got engaged on September 29 and we married on December 29. I don't know if I would recommend short engagements, and I guess some people might even consider ninety-two days to be a long one. But once the wedding was over, and our one-day honeymoon had come and gone, real life began to confront both of us. We realized that we really didn't know each other all that well.

In those first months of marriage, I saw that spending more time with my new wife was more important than going to Bible college. I felt that God told me to make my relationship with her a top priority.

One evening, my wife and I were talking with a member of a different religion about the fact that I was attending Bible college part-time. I explained that we had just been married, and that God had told me to spend more time with my wife. This person's jaw dropped, and he looked at me rather incredulously and asked, "Do you mean that God spoke to you?" I said, "In a voice that shook the house, no. But He did speak to my heart, and I knew what He wanted me to do."

I wish that there was an easy way or a surefire method that I could give you so that you could know God's will. In the times when I've felt that I knew what God wanted me to do, there was never any hard evidence — no recordings of God speaking from heaven and no witnesses who heard His voice. It was just a desire that I had, and I knew that God wanted to fulfill it. In each case, my wife had enough trust in God, and some in me, to know that everything would work out.

What I do know is that we need to be using our gifts and faithfully doing what's right in front of us. We might find out, as David did, that opportunities will present themselves to us as we go about our day. David wasn't looking for Goliath; he was just being faithful and doing his job. Even though he wasn't looking for it, his big break just showed up one day in the form of a very large Philistine.

And no matter what else God's will for us may include, one thing I know for sure is that He will want us to get out of our boats. Living in our comfort zones and doing great things for God are diametrically opposed. In order to accomplish God's will for our lives, we will have to get used to being asked to do things we've never done before. We'll have to learn how to live in the un-comfort zone, the area just beyond the current boundaries of what's comfortable for us. In other words, we'll have to learn to live by faith.

Keeping His Commandments

In 1 Samuel 13:13-14, God told Saul that his kingdom would not continue. Saul had often let fear make his decisions for him and the result was that he did things he shouldn't have done. In 1 Samuel 15, God told Saul to completely destroy Amalek and to kill everything that breathed. After the battle, Saul told Samuel that he had done all that God commanded him. Samuel replied, "Then why do I hear sheep?"

> *As the problems get bigger, so will your faith.*

Saul had not done as God commanded him, and rather than admit that he'd disobeyed God, he blamed the people. He said the people wanted to offer a sacrifice to God, so they saved the best of the sheep and oxen. In 1 Samuel 15:22 we read, "Has the LORD as great delight in burnt offerings and sacrifices, as in obeying the voice of the LORD? Behold, to obey is better than sacrifice."

During his reign as king, Saul did a lot of things wrong. But what ultimately cost him the kingdom was something that he didn't do. The problem was that he didn't obey God; he didn't keep God's commandments.

In the parable of the talents from Matthew 25, the master became angry with the servant who had received just one talent. He wasn't angry because the servant had lost the money. In fact, the servant still had his master's talent. The problem was that he hadn't done anything with what the master had given him. Like Saul, his problem wasn't what he did; it was what he didn't do.

Chapter 10: *The Conquering Life*

It was fear that led both Saul and the one-talent servant to disobey God. Saul seems to have been afraid of just about everything except God. He feared the Philistines, Goliath, and even his own people. The servant with the one talent was afraid that he'd fail and lose the talent. The sad thing is that both of them ended up losing all they had, not because they were reckless, but because they were fearful.

Faith and fear will always be battling for control of our thoughts. The one that wins will end up controlling our lives. It's up to us to meditate on God's word and learn to trust God in every circumstance we face. The day will come when we will stand before Jesus and give an account of what we did with the gifts and opportunities that God gave us. By letting fear run our lives, we risk losing all that we have.

The choice is ours. Do we want to be like the servant who received just one talent? Or do we want to be like the other two servants from the parable of the talents? Because they multiplied their talents, they were rewarded by God and heard Him say to them, "Well done, good and faithful servant; you were faithful over a few things, I will make you ruler over many things. Enter into the joy of your lord" (Matt. 25:21). The faithfulness that they had shown meant that they would be given great authority. They went from servants to rulers because they had used what they had received.

In 2 Corinthians 4:17-18 Paul says, "For our light affliction, which is but for a moment, is working for us a far more exceeding and eternal weight of glory, while we do not look at the things which are seen, but at the things which are not seen. For the things which are seen are temporary, but the things which are not seen are eternal." What we do with the circumstances we face in life will change something in us. It will work in us something that will last forever.

I hope that as you have read these characteristics from David's life you have found some tools and strategies that will help you make the most of the challenges you face in life. Whether you're facing a Goliath right now, or just a lion or a bear, know that God is there to help you. He has brought the exact circumstances into your life that can help you grow and move on to greater challenges and rewards. The struggles will never stop, and God's provision will never fail.

Like David, you will find that trusting God for big things will allow you to see His power displayed in your life. As the problems get bigger, so will your faith. As you wait on Him to fulfill His promises to you, He will strengthen and purify your faith. And when you stand before Him, you'll be able to say, "God, I did all that you told me to do. And I give You all the glory."

Appendix

1 Samuel 17

¹Now the Philistines gathered their armies together to battle, and were gathered at Sochoh, which belongs to Judah; they encamped between Sochoh and Azekah, in Ephes Dammim. ²And Saul and the men of Israel were gathered together, and they encamped in the Valley of Elah, and drew up in battle array against the Philistines. ³The Philistines stood on a mountain on one side, and Israel stood on a mountain on the other side, with a valley between them.

⁴And a champion went out from the camp of the Philistines, named Goliath, from Gath, whose height was six cubits and a span. ⁵He had a bronze helmet on his head, and he was armed with a coat of mail, and the weight of the coat was five thousand shekels of bronze. ⁶And he had bronze armor on his legs and a bronze javelin between his shoulders. ⁷Now the staff of his spear was like a weaver's beam, and his iron spearhead weighed six hundred shekels; and a shield-bearer went before him. ⁸Then he stood and cried out to the armies of Israel, and said to them, "Why have you come out to line up for battle? Am I not a Philistine, and you the servants of Saul? Choose a man for yourselves, and let him come down to me. ⁹If he is able to fight with me and kill me, then we will be your servants. But if I prevail against him and kill him, then you shall be our servants and serve us." ¹⁰And the Philistine said, "I defy the armies of Israel this day; give me a man, that we may fight together." ¹¹When Saul and all Israel heard these words of the Philistine, they were dismayed and greatly afraid.

¹²Now David was the son of that Ephrathite of Bethlehem Judah, whose name was Jesse, and who had eight sons. And

the man was old, advanced in years, in the days of Saul. ¹³The three oldest sons of Jesse had gone to follow Saul to the battle. The names of his three sons who went to the battle were Eliab the firstborn, next to him Abinadab, and the third Shammah. ¹⁴David was the youngest. And the three oldest followed Saul. ¹⁵But David occasionally went and returned from Saul to feed his father's sheep at Bethlehem.

¹⁶And the Philistine drew near and presented himself forty days, morning and evening.

¹⁷Then Jesse said to his son David, "Take now for your brothers an ephah of this dried grain and these ten loaves, and run to your brothers at the camp. ¹⁸And carry these ten cheeses to the captain of their thousand, and see how your brothers fare, and bring back news of them." ¹⁹Now Saul and they and all the men of Israel were in the Valley of Elah, fighting with the Philistines.

²⁰So David rose early in the morning, left the sheep with a keeper, and took the things and went as Jesse had commanded him. And he came to the camp as the army was going out to the fight and shouting for the battle. ²¹For Israel and the Philistines had drawn up in battle array, army against army. ²²And David left his supplies in the hand of the supply keeper, ran to the army, and came and greeted his brothers. ²³Then as he talked with them, there was the champion, the Philistine of Gath, Goliath by name, coming up from the armies of the Philistines; and he spoke according to the same words. So David heard them. ²⁴And all the men of Israel, when they saw the man, fled from him and were dreadfully afraid. ²⁵So the men of Israel said, "Have you seen

this man who has come up? Surely he has come up to defy Israel; and it shall be that the man who kills him the king will enrich with great riches, will give him his daughter, and give his father's house exemption from taxes in Israel."

²⁶Then David spoke to the men who stood by him, saying, "What shall be done for the man who kills this Philistine and takes away the reproach from Israel? For who is this uncircumcised Philistine, that he should defy the armies of the living God?"

²⁷And the people answered him in this manner, saying, "So shall it be done for the man who kills him."

²⁸Now Eliab his oldest brother heard when he spoke to the men; and Eliab's anger was aroused against David, and he said, "Why did you come down here? And with whom have you left those few sheep in the wilderness? I know your pride and the insolence of your heart, for you have come down to see the battle."

²⁹And David said, "What have I done now? Is there not a cause?" ³⁰Then he turned from him toward another and said the same thing; and these people answered him as the first ones did.

³¹Now when the words which David spoke were heard, they reported them to Saul; and he sent for him. ³²Then David said to Saul, "Let no man's heart fail because of him; your servant will go and fight with this Philistine."

³³And Saul said to David, "You are not able to go against this Philistine to fight with him; for you are a youth, and he a man of war from his youth."

³⁴But David said to Saul, "Your servant used to keep his father's sheep, and when a lion or a bear came and took a lamb out of the flock, ³⁵I went out after it and struck it, and delivered the lamb from its mouth; and when it arose against me, I caught it by its beard, and struck and killed it. ³⁶Your servant has killed both lion and bear; and this uncircumcised Philistine will be like one of them, seeing he has defied the armies of the living God." ³⁷Moreover David said, "The LORD, who delivered me from the paw of the lion and from the paw of the bear, He will deliver me from the hand of this Philistine."

And Saul said to David, "Go, and the LORD be with you!"

³⁸So Saul clothed David with his armor, and he put a bronze helmet on his head; he also clothed him with a coat of mail. ³⁹David fastened his sword to his armor and tried to walk, for he had not tested them. And David said to Saul, "I cannot walk with these, for I have not tested them." So David took them off.

⁴⁰Then he took his staff in his hand; and he chose for himself five smooth stones from the brook, and put them in a shepherd's bag, in a pouch which he had, and his sling was in his hand. And he drew near to the Philistine. ⁴¹So the Philistine came, and began drawing near to David, and the man who bore the shield went before him. ⁴²And when the Philistine looked about and saw David, he disdained him; for he was only a youth, ruddy and good-looking.

⁴³So the Philistine said to David, "Am I a dog, that you come to me with sticks?" And the Philistine cursed David by his gods. ⁴⁴And the Philistine said to David, "Come to me,

and I will give your flesh to the birds of the air and the beasts of the field!"

[45] Then David said to the Philistine, "You come to me with a sword, with a spear, and with a javelin. But I come to you in the name of the LORD of hosts, the God of the armies of Israel, whom you have defied. [46] This day the LORD will deliver you into my hand, and I will strike you and take your head from you. And this day I will give the carcasses of the camp of the Philistines to the birds of the air and the wild beasts of the earth, that all the earth may know that there is a God in Israel. [47] Then all this assembly shall know that the LORD does not save with sword and spear; for the battle is the LORD's, and He will give you into our hands."

[48] So it was, when the Philistine arose and came and drew near to meet David, that David hurried and ran toward the army to meet the Philistine. [49] Then David put his hand in his bag and took out a stone; and he slung it and struck the Philistine in his forehead, so that the stone sank into his forehead, and he fell on his face to the earth. [50] So David prevailed over the Philistine with a sling and a stone, and struck the Philistine and killed him. But there was no sword in the hand of David. [51] Therefore David ran and stood over the Philistine, took his sword and drew it out of its sheath and killed him, and cut off his head with it.

And when the Philistines saw that their champion was dead, they fled. [52] Now the men of Israel and Judah arose and shouted, and pursued the Philistines as far as the entrance of the valley and to the gates of Ekron. And the wounded of the Philistines fell along the road to Shaaraim, even as far as Gath and Ekron. ⁵³Then the children of Israel returned from chasing the Philistines, and they plundered their tents. ⁵⁴And David took the head of the Philistine and brought it to Jerusalem, but he put his armor in his tent.

⁵⁵When Saul saw David going out against the Philistine, he said to Abner, the commander of the army, "Abner, whose son is this youth?"

And Abner said, "As your soul lives, O king, I do not know."

⁵⁶So the king said, "Inquire whose son this young man is."

⁵⁷Then, as David returned from the slaughter of the Philistine, Abner took him and brought him before Saul with the head of the Philistine in his hand. ⁵⁸And Saul said to him, "Whose son are you, young man?"

So David answered, "I am the son of your servant Jesse the Bethlehemite.

Notes

1: Clarity — Preparing Our Hearts

1 Barbara Sher, *I Could Do Anything If I Only Knew What It Was* (New York: Dell, 1994), 52.

2 Maltz, Maxwell, Kennedy, Dan S. *The New Psycho-Cybernetics*, (New York: Penquin Putnam Inc., 2001), pp. 90-91

2: Challenge — Learning to be Faithful

1 Rohn, Jim, *The Treasury of quotes*, (Texas: Jim Rohn International, 2001), pg. 78

2 Eker, Harv, *Secrets of the Millionaire Mind*, (New York: HarperCollins Publishers, Inc., 2005), pg. 121

3 Rohn, Jim, *The Treasury of quotes*, (Texas: Jim Rohn International, 2001), pg. 91

4: Confrontation — Handling Criticism

1 Twain, Mark, Quoted in *Mark Twain Quotes*, http://www.mtwain.com/l_quotes2.html

2 Tracy, Brian, http://www.briantracy.com/main/articlesyndication.asp?ArticleID=65

6: Creativity — Using Our Imagination

1 Brown, Les, *It's Not Over Until You Win*, (New York: First Fireside Edition 1998)

7: Commitment — Making Decisions

1 Rohn, Jim, *The Treasury of quotes*, (Texas: Jim Rohn International, 2001), pg. 32

8: Courage — Facing Our Fears

1. Rohn, Jim, *The Treasury of quotes*, (Texas: Jim Rohn International, 2001), pg. 57

2. Mayo, Stacey, *I Can't Believe I Get PAID To Do This!*, (Georgia: Gold Leaf Publishing, 2004), pg 67

Bonus Offer

Are you ready to unleash the David in your life?

Simply go to:

www.Morgan-James.com/david

and sign up for a FREE 10-week email coaching course with Rob Marshall that will help you apply the principles you learned in this book.

At the website, you will also be able sign up to receive Rob's twice monthly newsletter and find information about other products and services that Rob offers.

Printed in the United States
56360LVS00002B/113